Carol Hewer

The Patchwork Point of View

JILL JARNOW

Simon and Schuster • New York

Published by Simon and Schuster
Rockefeller Center, 630 Fifth Avenue
New York, New York 10020

Designed by Jill Schwartz
Manufactured in the United States of America
Printed by The Murray Printing Company
Bound by American Book-Stratford Press, Inc.

1   2   3   4   5   6   7   8   9   10

Library of Congress Cataloging in Publication Data

Jarnow, Jill.
The patchwork point of view.
Bibliography: p. 157
1. Patchwork.   2. Applique.   I. Title.
TT835.J37   746.4'6   74-26974
ISBN 0-671-21957-X

Thank you to Susan White for getting me interested, to Lorraine Bodger for encouraging me to take the plunge, to Betsy Potter, Brenda Murphy, Melanie Zwerling, Victoria Rosenberg, and Kendra Adams for stitching with me and to Julie Houston for helping it all happen.

Special thanks to Rachel Newman and Herb Bleiweiss for the color photography.

For Al and his spirit of invention

CONTENTS

6 The Projects: A Matter of Interpretation

A COLOR SECTION FOLLOWS PAGE 64.

1

The Patchwork Point of View

AN OLD THEME WITH A NEW TUNE

Born out of a scrap bag from the desire to brighten existence, patchwork, appliqué, and quilting have survived through generations. But modern shortages and the drive for convenience threaten the spirit of this needlework. Delicately patterned, wonderfully workable cotton, once standard, is now disappearing from fabric shops. Today we are confronted with an avalanche of hard-to-handle, harshly designed synthetics. Lovingly stitched patchwork items are being replaced by those hastily assembled by mass production. Now, as we are deluged with all sorts of cheap, commercial imitations, the patchwork and quilting articles we produce with our own hands from thoughtfully chosen materials suddenly take on new importance. With the ever-pressing need to retain our identities, with the knowledge that quality materials are a vanishing species, and with many more leisure hours, we can turn to traditional techniques with renewed respect, joy, and hope. If we can adapt this stitchery and its many aspects of personal expression to our present-day needs, perhaps we can improve the quality of our lives.

Patchwork, appliqué, and quilting are refreshingly simple techniques. If you like a project that travels easily, and if you thrive on simple, satisfying involvements, try hand sewing. If you prefer quicker, but still charming results, use the sewing machine. In many cases, it is best to decorate a surface with hand stitching and to construct the finished item by machine. Hand stitching is warm and personal, and machine stitching is fast and durable.

Enjoy the traditional quilt, but let it suggest to you endless new directions. Consider combining differently patterned trims, fabrics, and appliqués when you make clothing. Add a special appliqué scene or patchwork cuff to wake up drowsy old denims. Decorate your walls with patchwork hangings. Cheer up a neglected kitchen with an appliqué utensil organizer.

Start your scrap bag collection today! Save old neckties and end pieces from sewing projects. Put in that old blouse if the style is tired but you still love the print. Indulgence is definitely allowed, so don't be afraid to buy new fabric for a special project or to add a few carefully chosen ribbons or patches to something you already have.

The patchwork, appliqué, and quilting projects in this book were made by a number of different craftspeople with individual styles and points of view. Design and needlework credits will be given along with the appropriate descriptive text for each project. The remaining pieces were made by me.

Please don't feel that any of the projects should be copied exactly. Happily, everyone's concepts, stitching, and choice of materials are wonderfully different. Interpret everything to fulfill your own inspirations and ideas. The projects were chosen to be useful, easy to make, and exciting to use. I hope everyone —from the beginner to the most experienced needleworker— will find them enticing and inspiring. Don't forget, most often the success of a project lies not in the intricacy of the tailoring, but in the selection and arrangement of the materials. New fabrics with old-time delicacy and charm are hard to find, so hunt and pick carefully. If you spend your time gathering materials that harmonize and setting stitches with love, you will find that you have created patchwork that sings a timeless tune.

USING THIS BOOK

Dedicated to the pleasures of sewing, the excitement of invention, and the joys of sharing, this book is for you. If you are just beginning to sew, you should find this book an encouraging, easy-to-follow introduction to patchwork, appliqué, and quilting. If you are more experienced, you might discover some suggestions and approaches that will help you to become more proficient. If you are already an expert, you could improve, or even change your outlook on what you sew. The techniques, concepts, and projects in this book are meant for everyone.

I hope that this book will guide you into areas of sewing that you have never visited. Turn to it for friendship and inspiration. Read through the sections on materials, work habits, and techniques, browse among the photographs and illustrations, and glance into the specific project descriptions.

When you are ready to begin work, read the appropriate sections again with care. If you are a beginner, tackle the easier, more explicitly described projects first. If you are experienced, you will be ready for the kind of improvisation that makes a finished piece distinctly yours. Consider again the sections on choice of materials and general concepts. You may feel that you prefer to work with more familiar approaches than those I have suggested. If something works well for you, use it. But always leave yourself open to new ideas offered by me or your other stitching friends. Don't reject a technique because you haven't heard of it before. After all, you'll never know until you try.

HISTORIC NEEDLEWORK:
LOOKING TO LEARN, LEARNING TO SEE

Look at old quilts! Visit museums and historical societies. Touch old quilts! Browse through antique shops and fairs. The most important reason to search for this traditional needlework is to see and feel for yourself why a quilt is beautiful. Although this is not a book on how to make quilts exclusively, much can be

learned by studying old bedcovers worked in patchwork, appliqué, and quilting. In today's predigested world it is necessary
to seek out and experience the old pieces to understand what
separates them from current, often thoughtlessly produced
needlework.

Quilts made in the United States, from the 1830s with
minute, subdued floral and geometric fabrics through the 1940s
with their lively colors and whimsical character, are easy to find.
See them on display in local historical societies as invaluable
household articles and hanging proudly in major museums as
revered works of art. Quilts are emerging from the attic in great
numbers and are for sale as respected antiques in shops around
the country. The fabrics of each decade, especially, have their
own unique, subtle qualities. Throughout the history of the
quilt, however, the beauty of geometric symmetry has prevailed,
providing the creator with both the visual pleasure of an orderly
system and a repeating structure to simplify work.

In the finest examples you will see the magical fusion of pattern, color, and needlework that is so often missing with today's
overabundance of commercial kits and mass-produced quilts.
Be warned, however, that the craftsmanship and use of materials of even the old quilts varies with each work. Don't forget
to stand away from what you are looking at to see how the
pieces fit together. Once you see the harmony of the techniques
and analyze the elements, you will want to incorporate the good
qualities into your own work and reject the bad.

REMEMBERING WHAT YOU SEE

Keep a record of what you see and build a reference file of designs. Make sketches of anything that you find exciting. No
matter how primitive your drawings, you could be jotting down
notes for a potentially fabulous creation. Record with the idea
of suggesting directions for yourself rather than duplicating
an object.

Clip and save any printed material from magazines, newspapers, or booklets that could possibly inspire you in the future. I have found my own reference file to be an invaluable source of direction. I browse through it for new ideas to begin a project as well as for suggestions once a project is in progress. Occasionally I will go into it for a clipping I remember having seen months before. When it turns up, I get a terrific feeling of satisfaction. When it doesn't (perhaps I didn't save that article after all) I experience a terrible letdown. As a result, I recommend storing away pictures as you see them. You'll be glad to have them eventually, whether it be tomorrow or in ten years.

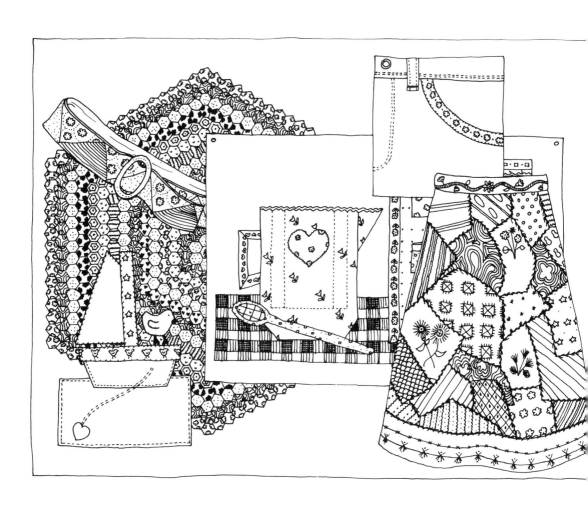

2

Home Sewing: The Spirit of Invention

IF YOU ARE JUST BEGINNING . . .

A positive attitude is probably the most important tool in the creation of your first patchwork or appliqué piece. Although you will be able to do many of these simple projects in less than an hour when you are an experienced needleperson, as a beginner you must forget about time. I recommend choosing a non-garment item for your first project because, in the beginning, it is important to avoid worrying about fit. If you work extremely slowly and carefully and consider this first undertaking as a learning experience, you will allow yourself to cope with the vital processes of appliqué hemming, patch registration, and layer quilting as they happen. These early, unhurried moments will help you to understand the value of each step. As you become more proficient, you will learn to cope with problems like shifting fabric and the manipulation of tiny appliqué shapes. You will learn how to take workable shortcuts, which will later reduce your working time considerably. When you feel the satisfaction of each completed piece, you will be eager for every new adventure.

17

I speak of the need for caution from experience. Several years ago, I jumped blindly, but confidently, into a patchwork project —theoretically a baby quilt. I was ignorant of the whole concept of patchwork, and, as work progressed, my project became uncontrollably lopsided. At the end of a few hours, the unfinished tangle was put into a paper bag for storage, never to be seen again. For years after, I harbored the idea that patchwork was one of those magical processes only for the very clever. But while I was busy being awed, many of my friends were busy patching, quilting, and appliquéing exciting clothes for themselves and fascinating needleworks for their environment. When I admired the wonders of a dress or a pillow, invariably its creator would exclaim "But it's so easy!" I would shrug my shoulders in despair and complain, "Maybe for you . . ."

Eventually I discovered some useful needlecraft books in the library. With their help, I bravely set off to reinvent sewing for myself. I began to discover solutions for what I had once considered insurmountable problems. I learned that careful choice and arrangement of materials, loving craftsmanship, and good humor can be combined to eliminate the need for time-consuming and painstaking tailoring. The ability to deal with these once-mysterious aspects of sewing in my own way has liberated me from the idea that sewing is a dry, uncompromising chore.

This personal discovery changed my creative outlook so much that I hope to be able to pass on the spirit of invention to you. No longer do I look at pieces of patchwork and appliqué wistfully. Now I look critically—for instruction and inspiration. If I can isolate the elements and decide where a piece of needlework succeeds or fails structurally and artistically, I can improve my own work.

Reading and looking can be educational, but actually doing something oneself is invaluable for learning. I have found this in my own experience putting together this collection of projects. I hope this experience can help you to get started stitching patchwork, appliqué, and quilting. That's good. But trade ideas with friends too and invent techniques that work best for you. That's great!

Defensive Sewing, or How to Prevent Panic Situations

The quality of stitching varies from person to person. Some people seem to take naturally to needle and thread. For others, it is a matter of lessons from friends, readings in craft books, and practice. The important thing, no matter what the level of your work, is to be neat. Sloppy stitching can interfere with and detract from the appearance of your finished work. Your stitches should reflect invention, excitement, and the pleasure you experienced while sewing your project. No matter how primitive, if your work is clean and uncluttered, you will be proud to have stitched it. It doesn't have to be dazzling to be worthwhile, but the stitching should not be more apparent than the work itself. This means you must learn to control frayed edges, to register patchwork increments, to conceal knots, to iron, and to ease out bulges. Some people feel so plagued by these "little annoyances" that they mistakenly believe that they cannot sew.

Fortunately, there are many precautions one can take to ensure that sewing sessions are smooth and unharried. Here is a list of some potential problem solvers. If you are one of those harassed needlepeople, check through to see if any of the suggestions below are appropriate to your situation. Most of these tips are discussed in further detail later.

1. Be calm, patient, and methodical as you work, and avoid cutting corners until you are skilled at the corners you are cutting. This will help you produce gracefully stitched, joyful needleworks.

2. Work on a clean, clear, flat surface. If nothing else is available, try cutting or assembling on the floor.

3. Invest in a pair of good, sharp scissors and save them for cutting fabric only. Once you use them, you will understand why they are a worthwhile investment.

4. Fit the tool to the task. Don't try to quilt with an oversized embroidery needle and don't try to fit six-strand floss into a tiny between-sized needle.

5. Choose materials that are clean, crisp, and durable. When using new fabrics, pick carefully. Avoid materials that are stained and tired looking while still on the bolt. Also reject fabrics that are loosely woven unless you are ready to joust with uncontrollable unraveling. On the other hand, fabric that is woven too tightly is hard to stitch. Set aside fabrics that are already stretched out of shape. They will never sit properly.

   Beautiful, old fabrics, usually hard to find, are sometimes available. If you use them, make sure ahead of time that they are strong enough to stand up to the function you have designated. If you are using recycled fabrics from used garments, choose only those areas that are still strong.

6. Analyze the weave of the material by holding it up to the light. When making patchwork or appliqué, place and cut fabrics, where practical, so they lie with the grain running in the same direction.

7. Always register—or align—your patchwork pieces with extreme care. Use straight pins to hold the pieces in place and double check to see that they are aligned before you sew. If you are new at patchwork, read the section beginning on page 39.

8. Always turn appliqué hems under, pin or baste them, and then pin or baste the appliqué shape in position on the base fabric before doing final sewing. This will prevent slipping.

9. Press all patchwork and appliqué projects in between steps.

10. Give all finished pieces a final pressing. Never, however, press quilting. Allow quilted pieces to follow the natural contours of the stitching.

Notes on Panic Situations or
What to Do When the Thread Tangles

The Aggravating Knot Never succumb to the temptation of yanking at a knot. You will immediately eliminate the chance to conquer it. You will want to pull hard—but don't. A little gentle probing will probably untangle it. The best thing to do is to stop and analyze the knot. If it is a snag with a small loop, insert the needle in the center of the loop and tug *gently* on one thread only. If the knot doesn't snap out, gently tug on the other end. Your thread will magically return to one smooth length.

If you find you have another kind of knot—the massive, hopeless-looking type, again, don't panic. I have found that if I use my needle and pluck very loosely at the mess, the whole mass will "untuck." Sometimes it takes a few tries to find that central point where all the tangling begins. Be sure to keep those exploratory efforts gentle so you will not aggravate the situation and you will give yourself time to reach the source of the problem.

Unfortunately, there are some knots that won't untangle, usually because they have been pulled before being recognized as knots. In these rare instances, there are three choices. You can cut off the knot and pull out enough stitching to be able to end off. Or, you can just keep sewing, knot and all. Some knots are so tiny that they will slide through the fabric with a tiny tug. Finally (and this is only if you can get away with it), you can conceal the knot under the fabric and continue working. Resort to this tactic only if you feel that you have a very good chance of success.

To avoid potential knotting, be sensitive to your thread. If you feel it beginning to twist out of control, pull on the loose end of the thread and let the needle dangle free. It will automatically untwist between your fingers and the piece you are stitching. This is one way to eliminate any knots before they bloom. I have found, however, that if I use quilting thread or bel-waxed cotton thread whenever possible, I have to deal with significantly less knotting. Use these thread types for all but the most delicate stitchery and you will be a happier stitchmaker.

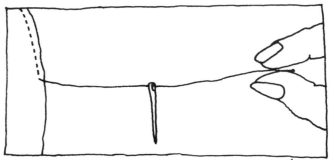

to avoid potential knotting pull on the loose end of the thread and let the needle dangle free between your fingers and your needlework

ON SEWING CLOTHES AT HOME

The pleasures and implications of sewing clothes from scratch at home are so positive that if you've never considered them before, you might be amazed. A friend who grew up with an aunt to sew her wardrobe explained the stigma she once felt from having clothes "homemade." Bette now feels, in reality, that her aunt sewed because she enjoyed it, not because of economic pressures. But as a child she thought that there was not enough money to buy clothes. She couldn't, without wearing store-bought garments, look like all the other children. Conformity was very important. As an adult, my friend now yearns for the excitement of being given something wonderful and individual to wear. But alas, her aunt is now sewing for some other lucky child.

Today, people respect and admire homemade clothing. How many times have you heard someone ask, in an awed voice, "Did you make that?" If you are an experienced needleperson you already know how satisfying it is to answer "Yes, I did." If you are a nonsewer you have probably felt let down if you had to answer "No, but my sister did."

Fortunately, it's never too late to learn to sew and to discover the joys of individuality. If you are a new sewer, read the section

"If You Are Just Beginning . . . ," on page 17, for some moral support. If you are already competent, look critically at your projects.

Have you been spending your valuable time (and never forget that it is) just making things when you could be inventing and creating them? As you develop control of techniques and learn to make conscious choices of materials, you will become more satisfied with your products and, as a result, increasingly independent of stylistic decisions made by clothing companies. Year after year, attractive, well-detailed clothing is disappearing from the reasonably priced shelf because it's becoming too expensive to produce. Next season's manufactured clothes will be more expensive and more shoddy than last. But by then you should be able to make a respectable amount of what you wear. Not only will you be creating some especially-you garments, but this new independence should enable you to put some of the money saved toward some well-made items you can't sew.

The Advantage and Pitfalls of the Commercial Pattern

The clothing in this book is based on easy-to-sew commercial patterns to be made special-to-wear by you. Depend on pattern companies for size and basic construction of a garment. But for personality and freshness, rely on yourself. Ordinary clothing is easy to produce using patterns. When you approach a pattern with ingenuity and invention you begin to have something worthy of the label "I made it." So take advantage of what these patterns have to offer but don't be dominated by the concept of saving time and don't be controlled by the sketch on the wrapper. Remember, commercial patterns are not the final word on the finished item but merely the skeletal framework of a never-before-thought-of garment. Choose your materials and plan your arrangements with care. Put in extra touches of appliqué and embroidery as you work. Patch in fabric changes where no one else would dare. Your finished creation should be unique, yet flattering. It should reflect you, its creator. After all, if it's going to look mass-produced, why sew it?

Commercial patterns can be priceless tools if you learn to dominate them with personal touches of your own. Get ideas for use of fabrics, texture, color, and placement of decorative stitching by scrutinizing beautiful clothing that you find in shops, museums, books, and magazines. Then, experiment with your own work by laying out all of your intended patchwork or appliqué materials to get an idea of how they sit together before you do any cutting. Aside from giving yourself a preview of the finished piece, you will also allow yourself an opportunity to rearrange and improve the color combinations within the confines of the pattern shape. It is during this period that you might do some important inventing.

Your patterns will remain surprisingly fresh if you fold and lightly iron them before you put them away. Because the same pattern can be interpreted so many ways, you may want to use a favorite many times. Through choice of materials, a kimono bathrobe and a casual spring wrap coat can both be produced from the same pattern pieces.

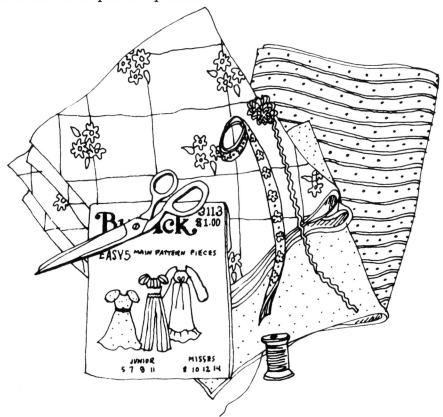

3

Fabrics: The Rainbow Quest

THE FINE ART OF FABRIC SHOPPING

The Fine Art of Fabric Shopping is a skill worth developing. Once you are able to walk fearlessly into the most muddled shop with the knowledge and endurance to determine what (if any) treasures it has to offer, you will know you have mastered this skill.

To begin your fabric collection, stake out those small, out-of-the-way yard goods shops with the best selection and the lowest prices. If you feel overwhelmed by the confusion of colors and patterns that predominate in many of these places, try to concentrate on locating printed cottons and cotton blends (herein referred to as just cotton). Fortunately, most stores keep them in an area by themselves, and once you find them you can eliminate everything else from your field of vision. Chances are, you will appreciate your purchases even more once you get them home and see that you have selected materials that add a very special, personal dimension to your work.

Don't forget the five-and-ten-cent store. To the amazement of my friends, that is where I have uncovered some of my favorite fabrics, hidden in a cluttered mass. Many discount and variety stores have fabric counters that carry an excellent selection of slightly damaged, low-cost cottons. Check each piece before you buy it to find the imperfection. Often it will be a nearly imperceptible misprint along the selvedge or some other minor problem. Of course, avoid badly disfigured materials. It will be no bargain if it detracts from the beauty of your finished piece.

Watch department stores for seasonal specials. But with the exception of these sales you won't find any great buys in department stores. What you might find is easy shopping and a good selection. Department stores keep up with the latest fashions, and since the trend in fabrics is a return to the traditional, you might find just what you need for patchwork and appliqué. Many people prefer department store shopping because it is so convenient. If you shop exclusively this way, you won't have to worry about damaged merchandise or running out of material. (Since small stores tend to carry end lots, once the bolt is gone it isn't replaced.) Admittedly, the services offered by a large store can't be duplicated by the smaller businesses, but be warned that if you neglect out-of-the-way places, you will eliminate a great deal of adventure and potential creativity from your life.

HOW TO CHOOSE COLORS

If you are planning a patchwork or appliqué project you might feel somewhat confused or overwhelmed about choosing a color theme. But selecting and arranging your fabrics with confidence is the key to personal, dynamic patchwork. I hope you will develop an adventurous attitude toward this particularly creative aspect of the sewing process. A woman I know has founded a small but thriving patchwork pillow business on her ability to use color. Though she uses only one or two basic patchwork shapes, her color arrangements are so vibrant that each pillow seems breathtakingly fresh. This is no accident. She hunts carefully from source to source for patterned fabrics. Then she experiments painstakingly with them until she finds the most exciting combinations. It's hard, but gratifying work. If you are at all ambivalent or afraid of combining fabrics, here are a few practice experiments I can recommend.

Even if you are not ready to buy, go to a shop that has a sizable selection of medium-weave cottons to experiment. Unless you have a particular aversion to the following color combination, look around the store and choose a red-white-and-blue print that you absolutely love. Consider carefully. Don't grab randomly at the first one you see unless you really like it. (By the way, many patterns with these colors predominating may have flecks of yellow, green, or other colors in them. Don't eliminate these, but if you want to maintain the red-white-and-blue motif, make sure one of those three colors always dominates). Once you have found a wonderful tricolor print, look around the shelves for other fabrics of similar weight made up of these colors. Most likely you will have several alternative combinations to play with. Not all red-white-and-blue patterns look good together. You will have to decide which ones do— and that is a very personal decision.

Set the fabrics you like best on a counter top or prop up the bolts in a quiet corner so they overlap each other. Consider the groupings from close up and far away. Try to imagine them sewn permanently together in smaller proportions.

If you like the result of this first exercise and really want to get in shape, look around the store and choose another fabric that catches your eye. Personal taste will be your best guide. Analyze the basic colors in this new piece. Choose what you want to emphasize and survey the store for bolts where these colors predominate. Experiment until you find fabrics that harmonize well with what you have already chosen. Try mixing ginghams, polka dots, and calico prints. Look for tiny geometrics and plaids.

The visual texture changes created by placing checks next to flowers, plaids, or dots can be very whimsical. Think about mixing different sizes of gingham, as Betsy Potter did with the Gingham Cat (see color section), but always combine materials of the same weight in a project. Arrange and rearrange fabrics with the same color feeling until you find two or three combinations that sing out to you.

If this is a buying trip, you should invest in small quantities (a yard each) of the fabrics in the combinations you love the best. These can later be used for patchwork. If you have already chosen a specific project to work on, of course you should buy the necessary amounts.

If you are planning a larger project and need to continue collecting in the same color vein, clip off small squares for reference when you get home. Keep them with you so you can find good companion pieces on your travels. These swatches are also good defense when trying to maintain your sanity in any chaotic yard goods shop. It's always wise to buy in combinations. You don't have to stick to these combinations when you get home if you find that you can then make an arrangement that you like better. In fact, many of your independent purchases will overlap. Don't be afraid to buy a random yard occasionally if you adore the print.

If you buy fabrics in advance and at your leisure you will be sure of always having terrific materials ready for patchwork and appliqué, and you will avoid that dejected feeling of having to make do at the last moment. Don't forget, by the way, to include in your fabric choices what you have saved in your scrap bag. Chances are good that with a little careful investigation, you will find that you have already collected many suitable materials.

If you are planning something for your environment or for someone else, consider where it will eventually reside. If you are planning something to wear, consider what you will wear it with. These references will help you make some of your color decisions by elimination. You will probably want to avoid making a pink-and-yellow patchwork confection for a room deeply committed to heavy wood and red, white, and blue. On the other hand, it's never too late to change your mind or develop new tastes, so don't stifle a potentially exciting project because it "won't go." Patchwork, wonderfully versatile and subtle, blends well with all types of decor. You'll be delighted when you discover how a few pieces of this vigorous needlework will revive a rigid or monotonous environment without overpowering it.

NEW OR OLD:SOME SPECIAL ADVICE

Many fabrics available today either are influenced by or are direct reproductions of charming old prints. Although such beautiful materials might at first seem hard to find, if you search from department store to yard goods shop to five-and-ten, you will be well rewarded. Cottons with a special ageless warmth are often hidden among those more abundant, poorly designed pieces.

One hundred per cent cotton, by the way, becomes scarcer every day. A small amount of synthetic fiber can keep a fabric looking fresh, but as the proportions shift to mostly man-made, the fabric becomes increasingly hard to handle. True cotton will hold the flat, clean crease that is so important to patchwork and appliqué. Artificial fibers will approximate this crease, but a polyester hem will always have a slightly rounded edge. To tell the difference between cotton and polyester, look at the cut edge of the fabric. Cotton of natural fibers will fray. The fibers in a piece of synthetic material will separate by falling away from the mass. Small appliqué shapes cut from synthetic fabric are almost impossible to control. If you have any further doubt about the content of a material give it a test pressing with a hot iron. Polyester, because it is Permanent Press, will almost always spring back to its original shape and the hot iron will stick to its surface.

Occasionally you will make an exciting discovery of old, never-used fabric, crisp, clean, and still on the original bolt. Most likely the fabric will be in fine shape, but examine it very carefully for weakness, rotting, or stains before including it in a project.

Be cautious when working with used materials. There is nothing more frustrating than watching a fabric split and fray uncontrollably before or soon after a project has been completed. There is definite value in saving an old set of curtains because they have outgrown their original usefulness, but beware of using favorite pajamas that have been machine washed and dried once a week for the last five years. The fabric is probably thin and tired. If you have retired a favorite blouse because of an accidental tear or a permanent stain and the rest of the garment is still strong, cut away the damaged area and save the rest.

Good things to save (provided, of course that there is still strength in the fiber) are: men's shirts and undershorts; all summer clothes including printed cotton dresses, blouses, scarves, and aprons. For crazy quilting, hold on to silk ties, scarves, and blouses. Save any discarded objects of lace, velvet, or fine wool. Save old tablecloths or bits of upholstery if they are covered with embroidery. If you plan to use old silk or woolen ties for a Victorian creation, make sure they will not be expected to do heavy-duty work. Silk, especially, does not age well and has a tendency to split. Basic tie patterns, fortunately, have remained subdued and tasteful over the years while tie widths have fluctuated. These newer fabrics would be a good choice for a crazy quilt skirt or handbag (as shown in color section), while the older ties could be saved for a special occasion coverlet or something under glass.

Don't limit your scrap bag acquisitions to your immediate surroundings. If you are an active crazy quilter, you should always be on the lookout for fancy materials. Neckties, especially, are discarded fairly frequently. There is nothing more exciting to the former owner than to see an old tie incorporated into a magical piece of patchwork.

Washing

Patchwork objects made of cotton may be washed in cool water by hand or in a machine set to a gentle cycle. If you have combined pure cotton with cotton blend fabric or you have combined old and new fabrics, consider dry cleaning because the materials within your piece will shrink at different rates.

After washing, patchwork pieces should be hung to drip dry and then lightly ironed. Quilted articles should not be ironed however. Instead they should be allowed to remain as they dry —in their natural contour.

Crazy quilt projects or anything containing an unidentified material should be dry-cleaned.

4

Tools and Toys

BASIC SUPPLIES

Thread

For all-purpose machine and hand sewing, I prefer standard mercerized cotton or bel-waxed thread. Polyester is hard on my hands and seems to fight the machine. Many people, however, prefer polyester. Its advantages include a wide range of colors and general availability.

If you do a lot of machine sewing, especially satin stitch machine appliqué, you already know how quickly one goes through a spool of thread. This can become surprisingly expensive. One way to save money is to use basting thread for all temporary stitching. In addition to being very economical, it is a great frustration preventative, and it is easy to remove without risk of injuring fabric. Use lightweight basting thread for all preliminary appliqué hemming and tacking and see how much you save.

Special quilting thread is waxed heavy-duty cotton that will glide through layers of fabric and filler and will resist snarls. Unfortunately, the color range is limited, and it is also hard to find in local stores. However, it is available through mail order houses listed on page 36.

Embroidery floss is fun for decoration. It comes in beautiful colors and adds a special dimension to crazy quilting, as seen in the color section. Use it straight from the skein, six strands at a time, or separate the strands for more delicate work.

Yarn is also wonderful for decorative stitchery. But always use high-quality yarn for your work. Cheap yarn detracts from the way your work looks and wears out quickly—sometimes even as you are stitching.

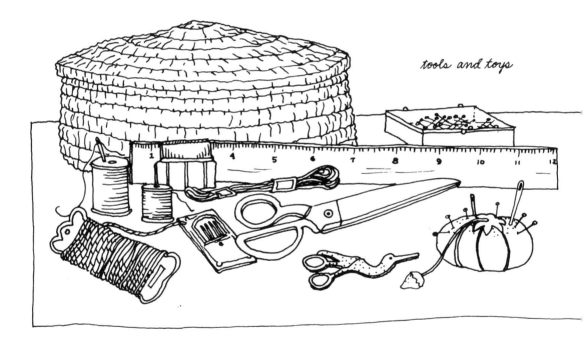

tools and toys

Scissors

When working with patchwork and appliqué, it is especially important to make clean, accurate cuts, because the pieces are often small and clean edges are critical. Scissors that chop rather than cut are the most frustrating hindrance in the world. Use sharp, nine-inch cutting shears and save them for cutting fabric only. Paper will dull the blades.

Small embroidery scissors are terrific for snipping threads and making small cuts.

You will also need a pair of all-purpose scissors for cutting paper patterns and anything else.

Pins

Use medium-sized straight pins. Avoid super-fat ones; they can leave permanent marks. Beware of tiny ones because they are hard to handle. Discard bent pins; they won't do their job. I prefer working with pins with plastic heads because they are easy to see and nice to touch.

Pincushion

Whether you make your own or use the traditional strawberry, a pincushion helps you keep track of your pins and needles. Don't overload your pincushion or it will be hard to use. Fill it with just what you need for an average project and keep the others stored away. By the way, the little bud dangling from the standard strawberry cushion is filled with rosin. Run your pins and needles through it to keep them clean.

Thimble

A thimble feels incredibly extraneous and awkward at first, but, as you start pushing that needle through layers of fabric, you will appreciate the extra protection. I wear my thimble on the middle finger of my sewing hand. When buying your first thimble, try on several until you find one that fits snugly without pinching.

Needles

Choose the right needle for the right chore and it will make the job easier. Numbers 7–10 "betweens" are good for quilting and for all-purpose sewing. Numbers 3–9 are good for embroidery and appliqué. Most important is to use what feels comfortable. However, don't be "trapped" by what you are used to without giving something else a fair try. Comfortable with large tapestry needles used for needlepoint, for a long time I resisted using small needles, thinking them hard to handle. After a few sessions of quilting with a tiny between-sized needle, I began to realize how well suited it was to quilting. Now I make the adjustment from needlepoint to quilting with ease.

Marking Tools

Tailor's chalk comes in dark and light shades and is great for marking on fabric.

A medium lead pencil is also good.

Dressmaker's carbon and a tracing wheel are also useful for transferring appliqué and quilt patterns. Be sure to use a color of carbon that will be visible on the fabric.

Templates

A template is a cardboard pattern. Shirt cardboard is especially good because it can be cut easily with scissors or an X-Acto knife. If you are working with a shape that repeats many times, you may need replacement templates. Cardboard corners and edges wear out.

Although I have never used it, sandpaper can be used if you are having trouble with slipping fabric. Use the rough side against the material.

Blotter paper or index cards can also be used.

Glue

Fabric glue is good for tacking hard-to-pin trims like rickrack. It is wonderful for use on nonapparel items like the Button Pictures shown in the color section, but, if you are making a garment that will be washed or cleaned, don't rely on it to be permanent. Always sew over it.

Spray adhesive is magic. It goes on easily, allows shifting while still wet, sticks indefinitely, and won't soak through fabric. It is, of course, also meant for nongarment articles. Always use spray glue in a well-ventilated room and carefully cover everything but the area to be sprayed. The fumes are terrible and the glue is an impossible nuisance when it falls on an unintended surface. Be sure to read the directions and the warnings on the can.

Iron

Use an iron to keep your patchwork and appliqué projects under control as you work. Iron each new patchwork addition flat and steam the hem of an appliqué shape before sewing it down.

Use a press cloth between your iron and the object to prevent scorching, or consider using an iron with a Teflon-coated bottom. Always do your pressing on the underside of the fabric to avoid marks.

Keep a spray can of water nearby for steaming. Even if your iron makes its own steam, you will probably need more than it can give.

Commercial Patterns

Obviously the choice of commercial patterns depends on the person and the project. For a discussion of how to use commercial patterns to their best advantage turn to page 23.

SPECIAL SHOPPING INFORMATION

Needles, thread, fabric, and scissors are such standard items that if you don't already own them, you should have no trouble finding them wherever you are in the world. Almost every sewing supply can be found in your local variety store. For a detailed discussion of purchasing and collecting fabrics, turn to "The Fine Art of Fabric Shopping" on page 25.

Unfortunately, certain articles—like special quilting thread, Dacron batting, and quilting hoops—can be difficult to locate. Search determinedly through your local craft supply shops and department stores. Salespeople may be unaware of a product, but that doesn't mean that it can't exist or that it isn't buried somewhere among the shelves. Persist! If all else fails, consider these mail order houses.

Herrschners, Inc., Hoover Road, Stevens Point, Wisconsin 54481

Lee Wards, Elgin, Illinois 60120

J. C. Penney Company, Catalog Division, 11800 West Burleigh Street, Milwaukee, Wisconsin 53263

Sears, Roebuck and Company, 4640 Roosevelt Boulevard, Philadelphia, Pennsylvania 19132

WORK SPACE

Try to provide yourself with an efficient storage and work space. Especially if you are planning a large project like a quilt or curtains, you will need a spacious, unencumbered surface for at least the cutting and assembling. If a work space simply isn't available as a permanent arrangement, clear away a spot on the floor for temporary use. However, since you will always want to use your sewing machine at a table, you will have to find at least a medium-sized desk for this.

For my own work area I acquired a hollow door and painted it white. It is supported by an old cast-iron Singer sewing-machine base at one end and industrial bookshelves at the other. A nice, sturdy, alternative support would be sawhorses from the

organizing a work space

lumberyard painted white or a bright, shiny color. For lighting I clamped a gooseneck lamp to the edge of the desk top and for seating I used an old wooden office chair. It's comfortable, adjustable, and fun to swivel. I keep needles, thread, pins, bobbins, and thimbles in a small covered basket and fabrics in a large wicker hamper. An empty jam jar with an intriguing English label holds my pencils, scissors, tape measure, and fabric glue within easy reach. Inexpensive clear plastic boxes from the five-and-ten-cent store are also invaluable to my storage system. They allow me to keep my treasured trimmings organized and always in view. The compartmented, hardware size displays buttons and ribbons, and the shoebox size protects assorted fruits, flowers, and packages of rickrack.

Other containers I have lovingly collected for my studio include a cookie tin covered with fabric, for sewing scraps; a clean, heavy-duty fruit crate, with a beautiful, old-fashioned label, for housing fabrics in use (and an occasional cat that jumps in for a short nap); round glass honey jars, for beads; and a small, plastic strawberry carton with ribbon threaded through the mesh, for catching small, in-progress pieces.

Two wooden cola crates painted white hang directly over my worktable. Perched in them are my pincushion, bead jars, button and ribbon boxes, thread, and any fun things I have accumulated.

As you can see, my demands for a work space emphasize utility, invention, and pleasure, rather than cost. I have painted the walls and many of the objects white to allow the color of my tools and projects to dominate. In fact, when a project is in progress or newly completed, I often tack it to the edge of the cola crate or to the wall so I can enjoy it. Many times, seeing a piece of needlework in an unguarded moment helps suggest improvements and new directions. It also gives me a feeling of accomplishment and pride while adding its own decorative touch to the entire area.

5

The Techniques: Thoughts for Hand and Heart

PATCHWORK

Patchwork is the technique of joining small pieces of fabric together with seams to make a larger unit. Most often made of square increments which are sewn to each other, patchwork items are considered to be "pieced" together. Patchwork articles such as the tablecloth on page 102 are usually divided into regular block parts to simplify design organization and sewing. Each small piece is joined to another until a large block is formed. A patchwork project usually consists of many small blocks or patches. In quiltmaking, the process of joining these modules to form the top layer is called "setting" the quilt.

Materials

All the patchwork projects in this book are made from medium-weave prints, plaids, checks, and solids in cotton. Durable cotton, although becoming scarce (see page 29), is easy to sew, comfortable to use, and comes in a rainbow of colors, patterns, and weights. Use a variety of cotton fabrics in colors of your choice, but be sure to keep the weight of the fabrics equal within each project, or be prepared to battle uneven tension and puckering. Test wash any fabric that you suspect might run or shrink—or plan to have the finished article dry-cleaned.

The Plan

If you chart out your complete, intended patchwork design on a piece of paper before you begin work, you will prevent possible mistakes later. You will know ahead of time how many pieces of what colors you must prepare to fulfill your design plan. Aside from saving time, you also save yourself potential aggravation. There is nothing so frustrating at the end of a hard day's work as the discovery that you are missing several pieces to complete your pattern or that you haven't enough fabric on hand.

Pressing

Press all of your intended material, even the tiny pieces, on the wrong side before you begin work. This will ensure accurate cutting and easy stitching. Continue to press your work in between steps to keep new additions under control.

The Template

The template is a cardboard pattern. Cut to the actual dimensions of a patchwork increment, it is traced on to fabric to provide the sewing line. When tracing, be sure to leave adequate space between shapes for seam allowances. You will need a separate template for each basic module within your patchwork project.

Draft your patchwork shape with a pencil and ruler on a piece of paper. Try using graph paper for extra guidance. Convert your shape into a usable template by transferring it to shirt cardboard, blotter paper, index paper, or sandpaper. You may

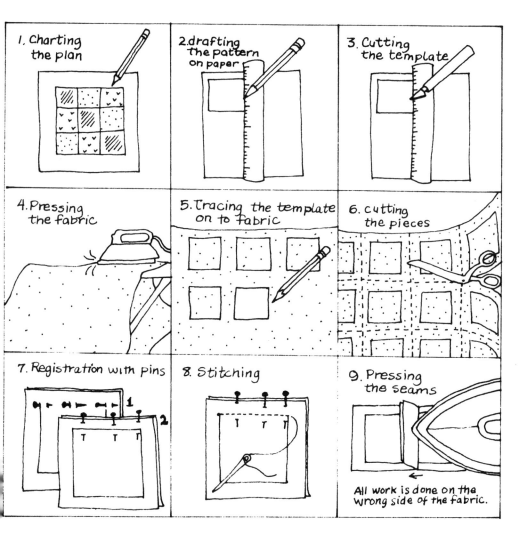

1. Charting the plan

2. drafting the pattern on paper

3. Cutting the template

4. Pressing the fabric

5. Tracing the template on to fabric

6. cutting the pieces

7. Registration with pins

1
2

8. Stitching

9. Pressing the seams

All work is done on the wrong side of the fabric.

patchwork procedure

trace the drafted shape onto the stiffer surface with a ruler to guide you by sandwiching carbon paper between the original and the cardboard. Tape the original and the cardboard to a table top and slip the carbon in between. This will assure you of strong, clear lines. Using scissors or an X-Acto knife and ruler, cut out the patchwork template exactly along the lines. You can skip the transfer process if you draw your pattern with a pencil and ruler directly on the cardboard.

Using the Template

Place your fabric on a hard surface *with the wrong side up.* Secure the template with one hand, also wrong side up, and trace around it with a medium pencil or chalk. This will be your sewing line. Make sure the template sits on the fabric with one edge running parallel to the grain to prevent puckering and pulling later when the many patchwork increments are joined. When your first shape is outlined, move the template over and repeat. Continue tracing until you have fulfilled your plan with the right shapes in the right colors.

Tracing and Cutting

Place these shapes on the fabric economically so a minimum will be wasted in the cutting. Be very careful, however, to leave one-half inch between the shapes. Cut out the patchwork pieces one-quarter inch from the drawn stitch lines. The extra quarter inch of fabric will be the seam allowance.

Joining the Pieces

Sew the patchwork pieces together two at a time using a tiny running stitch. Place two adjoining shapes together face to face, register them carefully with pins (as described on page 70), and sew along one seam. Take a backstitch at the beginning and end of each sewing line for strength. Press the pairs open on the wrong side, with both seams pressed to one side rather than open. This will minimize the strain on the stitching. Continue by joining pairs together into whole strips, and press again. Finally, hem the strips together to form the larger unit. Check to see that all strips are accurately aligned before doing final sewing. When a block is complete, press again on the wrong side with the seams to one side.

Where to Begin

For the most instructive introductory patchwork experience and more written details, try completing the Basic Patchwork Quilted Pillow, which begins on page 65. Don't forget, because the pattern of the Basic Patchwork Pillow is so simple, that it will be your inventiveness, choice of materials, and stitching that will give the finished piece warmth, charm, and vitality.

PARALLEL-STRIP PATCHWORK

Parallel-strip patching is a wonderful way to create a very basic patchwork fabric without a template or tedious registration. The resulting patched piece can be used as a foundation for many projects. The Patchwork Bears on page 107 are both dressed in strip-patched outfits. The doll on page 113, the turtle on page 106 and the summer bag on page 120 are constructed with the parallel-strip-patch method. But these are just the beginning. See what you can devise using the parallel-strip patching. It will be the fastest patchwork project you ever made.

To make parallel-strip patches, snip a small straight line with sharp scissors into the selvedge, or bound edge, of a length of cotton. With a smooth, continuous motion, tear across to the facing selvedge. The resulting edge will be straight and clean. If you tear lengthwise instead, the fabric will put up a good fight and the torn edge will be puckered and uneven. If you have a scrap of cotton with no apparent selvedge, hold it up to the light. The strands that run parallel to the selvedge will appear heavier. *Always tear against these.*

As with other patchwork projects, always press your strips before sewing. Then, to sew, place two strips face to face, without pinning. Be careful to keep the torn edges of both even on the side where they are to be stitched. If you do this, the strips will always be parallel when you are done. Run the strips through the machine, keeping the presser foot aligned with the ragged right edge, or sewing edge. Sew the strips in pairs as you would with other patchwork. In fact, all other patchwork rules apply to parallel-strip patchwork, so read the patchwork section which begins on page 39 for more hints.

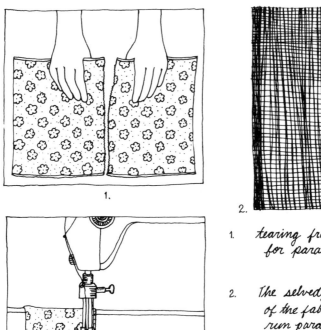

1. *tearing from selvedge to selvedge for parallel-strip patchwork*

2. *The selvedge is the bound edge of the fabric. The strands that run parallel to the selvedge appear heavier.*

3. *using the presser foot to align parallel-strip patches*

APPLIQUÉ

Appliqué is the method of layering one piece of fabric on top of another and sewing it permanently in place. The materials, shapes, and stitches may vary from project to project, but the process is constant: cutting, hemming, pressing, placing in position, and sewing down. Soft, medium-weave cottons like calico, gingham, and muslin are best because they are easy to cut and hem. Beware of cotton blends that are mostly synthetic fibers. These will not hold a press and, therefore, are difficult to mold into appliqué shapes. If you substitute felt as your material or use machine zigzagging instead of hand stitching, the hemming process will be eliminated. The finished product, however, will be less traditional than a piece hand-stitched on cotton. Here is a basic outline for completing the appliqué projects in this book.

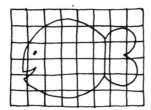

Enlarging Drawings

When you want to enlarge a drawing from this book or any other source, rule a grid of equal-size squares over a tracing of the original artwork. Next, rule off squares of a larger dimension, but an equal proportion, on another sheet of paper. If you want to enlarge a drawing to twice its original size, draw the first grid of ¼-inch squares and the enlargement grid of ½-inch squares. If you want to enlarge something two-and-a-half times from the ¼-inch grid (also interpreted as ⅜-inch), the enlargement squares should measure ⅝ of an inch.

To draw the enlargement, look carefully to see where the original crosses the lines of the small grid. Then mark off every place where the original crosses the lines of the small grid in the same location on the enlargement grid. Using the original drawing for reference, connect the marked-off dots on the enlargement grid.

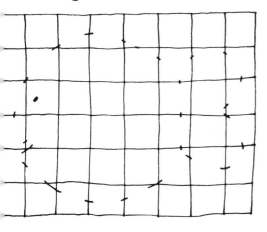
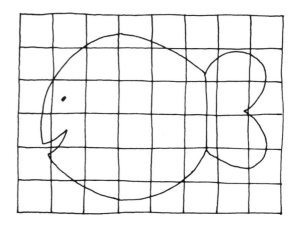

Making a Template

You will need to make a template, or pattern, to transfer a design to fabric. A template is especially useful if you intend to repeat the shape several times. Place a piece of carbon paper between your original—whether it is an enlargement or a drawing of your own—and a sheet of shirt cardboard, index paper, or blotter paper. Tape the original over the cardboard to make the job easier and slip the carbon between them. Go over the lines of the original with a firm pencil line. Next, cut out the cardboard shape along the lines.

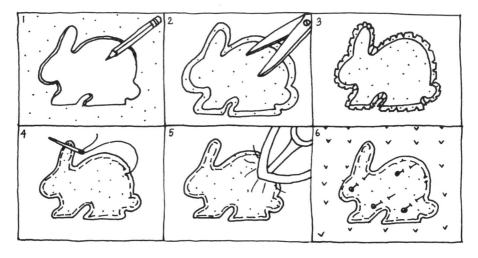

APPLIQUÉ PROCEDURE:

1. tracing the template onto fabric
2. cutting out the shape 1/4" from the outline
3. cutting notches in the curves
4. basting under the hem
5. pressing the hem
6. pinning shape in position on backing fabric

Using the Template

Place the template *right side up on the right side of the fabric.* Securing it with one hand, trace around it with a medium pencil or chalk so the outline is visible on the fabric.

Cutting the Appliqué Shape

For accurate cutting you will need sharp scissors with at least four-inch straight blades. Cut the appliqué shape ¼ inch out from the traced line. This extra ¼ inch all around is the hem allowance.

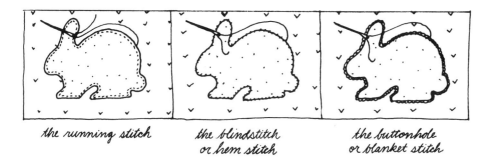

the running stitch   the blindstitch   the buttonhole
                            or hem stitch   or blanket stitch

Hemming

With the tracing facing you, use your thumb and index finger to fold under the hem allowance. Your fold should include the tracing line. If you are doing this correctly, you will be folding away from you.

Using a running stitch (see page 49) with the knot on the top of the shape for easy removal later, firmly baste the edges under as you fold. If the appliqué shape is rounded, you will have to snip notches in the curves for easy and accurate folding. To make these notches, clip in at each turn, right up to the seam line—but not through it. If the shape has corners, you will have to miter them so they will fold neatly.

Hemming—an Alternate Method

Many people find basting time-consuming and annoying; they prefer pinning appliqué hems in place. If the shape is large and simple, I can understand the time-saving advantages of this alternate method. But, aside from losing valuable control with the pin approach, I have never managed to sew around the pins without jabbing myself painfully. Moreover, if a shape is at all intricate, it requires so many pins to keep the edges under that I find pins blocking every stitch. Needless to say, this is not one of my favorite methods, but, because it is so widely used, I present it to you on the chance that you can make it work.

Pressing

If you have basted your hem under, apply steam to it on the wrong side of the shape to make it more secure for permanent sewing. If you have used the pin method, place a cloth between the shape and the iron before you press.

Pinning in Position

Because the appliqué pieces tend to slip as they are being sewn down and you almost never realize it until all of the intricate sewing has been done, I do advocate pinning shapes on to the base fabric in exact position. If your patch is big, use at least three pins to avoid shifting. Place the pins in the interior of the shape to keep from being jabbed. If the appliqué is small, consider basting it in place or hold the shape with your thumb and check the placement as you work to correct any movement. If you have pinned the edges under in your preliminary hemming, rather than basting, reinsert some of the pins so they tack the appliqué to the base fabric.

Sewing in Place

All of the steps discussed so far have been meant to make this final process so unharried that you will be able to concentrate on making even, artful stitches. Methods and stitch preferences vary, so again, I present my favorites to you. Examine finished pieces of needlework as you see them on display in shops or elsewhere in your travels to see what you prefer visually. Then make stitch experiments to discover what technique you enjoy. Naturally, depending on which is most comfortable, these decorative stitches can be worked from the left or the right.

Blindstitch or Hemstitch

The blindstitch or hemstitch is strong, attractive, and fun to do. Bring your needle up from the underside of the fabric through the appliqué shape close to the edge, and down again outside the edge, on the back fabric. The downstroke pierces the backing material but not the appliqué. Whether your stitches are on a slant or at right angles to the appliqué edge, make sure to be consistent once you have established the size and direction. Stitch lengths may vary from nearly invisible to one inch long, depending on your inclination. The important thing is to catch the hem in your stitching process.

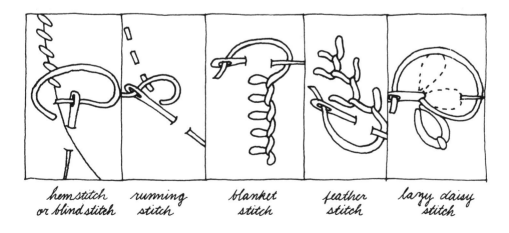

hemstitch   running   blanket   feather   lazy daisy
or blind stitch   stitch   stitch   stitch   stitch

The Running Stitch

The running stitch is another popular method because it is fast and strong. If you use this technique, make sure to sew within the hem allowance so the fabric folded under will be fastened by the stitching.

The Buttonhole or Blanket Stitch

These two stitches add an extra bit of elegance and strength to your appliqué. You may fasten the shape first with a medium running stitch or work directly on a pinned appliqué. Make blind stitches, but loop the thread below the needle on each stitch. If you place your upright strokes close together, you will be buttonholing. If you leave a wide space you will be making blanket stitches.

More Stitches

Other decorative stitches that you might enjoy include the feather stitch and the lazy daisy. See the section on Crazy Quilts, page 64, for additional stitches.

Materials and Visual Impact

Your stitching will be delicate or forceful, depending on the kind of thread you use and the size, consistency, and choice of stitches. Choose from sewing thread, embroidery floss, or yarn. Whether you use large running stitches or compact buttonholes, be aware that every decision you make in the use of your materials and stitching, on purpose or by accident, will have its own particular visual impact.

Appliqué by Machine

Appliqué may also be done by machine, although machine-stitched pieces have a totally different visual and tactile feeling from those that are hand-stitched. The results can be a pleasant change however. Machine stitching has its own whimsical flavor while offering the advantages of strength and fast results.

Straight Stitching   If you are working with large, simple shapes, you may machine straight stitch around a hem that has been basted or pinned on a backing fabric. Because this method is extremely durable, it was used to make the Appliqué Kitchen Catchall on page 82.

MACHINE APPLIQUÉ:

cut shapes to the stitch line   zigzag to appliqué
and pin in position

Zigzag or Satin Stitching   You may also use machine zigzag stitches to appliqué. Cut your shapes right to the sewing line and pin them in place. Set your machine for zigzag stitches and run your piece through. Make sure these stitches have a good grip on the edges of the appliqué shape or it will separate later. For safety, I recommend keeping at least three-quarters of the stitch on the appliqué shape. Machine satin stitching uses an extraordinary amount of thread, so make sure to have a good supply of the color you are using when you sit down to work. Both the Easy Appliqué Satchel on page 118 and the Houses-by-the-Sea Appliqué Quilt on page 95 were done with this stitch.

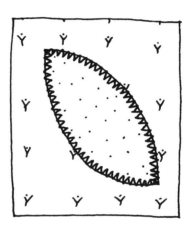

Unusual Appliqué

Anything that can be stitched to the surface of fabric should be considered for appliqué—from ribbon and old pieces of lace to fabric flowers, leather scraps, pieces of crochet, beads and buttons. Remember, of course, to think about durability and washability when assembling materials for clothing.

Old buttons as appliqués hold a magical fascination for me. As a result, I collect old buttons as I see them because many, I know, I will never see again. Compare an old glass or plastic button to its present-day counterpart and you will see a subtle (and sad) difference in quality. You may even begin to understand the excitement I feel about the old, whimsically shaped, delicately decorated buttons. Be assured that it isn't necessary to purchase these little treasures in large quantities unless you have a specific project. You may, of course, decide to revive a tired work shirt or blouse by changing the buttons, or you may suddenly find some that you really love. Unless this is the case, invest in them by the pair. You'll be surprised how many ways you'll invent to use them—as a special trim on an appliqué garment, as a facial feature in a patchwork toy, in a button picture, or in their ultimate state as an art form. But place your buttons with care. Inappropriately used buttons can ruin a project.

To me, buttons are in the small-sculpture category. If you feel as I do, treat them with respect, as treasures in themselves, or as a part of a greater creation. Devise a permanent display for your favorite buttons by sewing them to a quietly elegant piece of velvet in a carefully considered, symmetrical design. Or let the theme of your buttons suggest a patchwork, quilted, appliqué environment. Subjects I particularly enjoy working with include still lifes with fruit and flower buttons and landscapes with animals. For directions, turn to page 86.

Cotton ribbons also make wonderful appliqués because they are so beautiful and need no hemming. The price of ribbon fluctuates so much from small shops to department stores that I usually buy extra amounts if I find an especially pretty ribbon at an inexpensive price.

QUILTING

Quilting is the technique that joins together three layers of material to make a warmer, stronger fabric. The basic quilt stitch is simple. It's nothing more than a tiny running stitch. The hard part is learning to control and gauge the size and placement of stitches while producing a smooth, evenly stitched bedcover. With practice and concentration you can discover how to quilt well.

For faster results and a more contemporary look, quilting may also be done with a sewing machine.

The layers of a bedcover can also be joined together by "tufting" or "tying." This technique is most often seen joining two layers rather than three. It is described on page 64.

USE QUILT STITCHING:

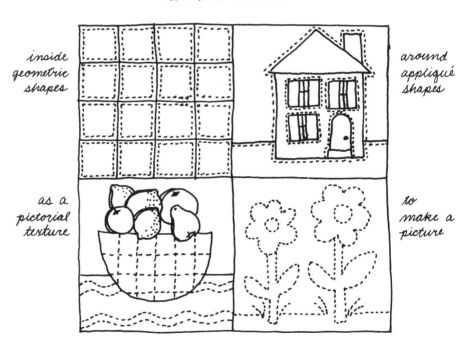

inside geometric shapes

around appliqué shapes

as a pictorial texture

to make a picture

Where to Quilt

Quilting stitches may be set parallel to the outside of the edge of an appliqué to emphasize the silhouette or placed inside an appliqué to describe texture or features. If you are quilting a geometric top, stitch around or through the inside contours of each patch.

Pattern Transfer

Quilting may be done by eye or with the aid of a chalked pattern. If you are quilting something with geometric edges and want help, use a ruler to make chalked or penciled guidelines. If you are planning a more elaborate quilt design, first draw it to scale on brown paper. Perforate the lines with a tracing wheel, needle, or unthreaded sewing machine. Pin your perforated plan in position on your quilt top. In a color visible on the fabric to be quilted, rub in chalk until it shows on the top material. Quilt along the lines. When quilting has been completed you can remove the chalk by brushing it off or by dry cleaning.

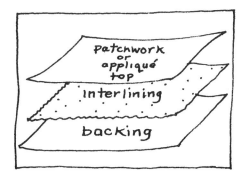

The Layers

Three layers make up the sandwich to be quilted. The top may be patchwork, appliqué, a combination of both, or a plain sheet of material. The type of top you choose will influence the stitch

placement. The center layer (or interlining) can be flannel or
a light blanket. Most popular, however, is polyester batting,
which comes in rolls measured to standard bed sizes. The backing material should be soft, medium-weave cotton; you may
either piece it to size or use a precut bedsheet. When assembling
a quilt make sure the interlining and the backing are slightly
larger than the top sheet.

If you have chosen lightweight materials for each of your
layers, you will find quilting a breeze. But if you try to quilt a
heavily layered top or tightly woven fabric, the bulk will give
you trouble. Setting the stitches evenly is tricky when you have
to struggle to push the needle and thread through the layers. If
you want to make a bedcover from an appliquéd sheet, crazy
quilt top, or any other difficult material, consider "tufting" as
described on page 64.

Placement of Layers

Getting the layers to sit evenly before you baste them together
is important. If you are working on a quilt this could be a battle
of the bulge, but if you are working on a small bag or pillow you
shouldn't have much problem.

Lay the backing out first on a hard, flat, clear area, face down.
Consider taping the edges down. Spread the interlining directly
over it, smoothing out any lumps. Place the decorative top face
up over the other layers. Center it. Working from the middle,
gently smooth the three layers with your hand so there is an
extra margin of lining and backing sticking out from under the
top sheet on all sides.

Pinning and Basting

Pinning and basting the layers together before you begin to quilt
are two invaluable defensive precautions. If you fasten the layers
firmly now, you won't have to worry about shifting fabric. Always start from the center of the piece and work toward the

corners. When you are satisfied that you have pinned in enough places and the layers won't shift, you may begin to baste. If you are working on something as large as a quilt you will be doing a lot of basting, so consider using a basting thread. It's economical and it's easy to remove. Save your more expensive quilting thread for permanent stitching. Basting, by the way, may soon get in the way of your quilt stitching, so don't hesitate to snip it away as soon as it has become obsolete. But take out only what's necessary or you will be left with three layers of potential quilt flopping out of control. Basting, as with pinning, and later, quilting, should be started at the center of your piece and worked toward a corner. When you reach the corner, end off and begin again in the middle. Always ease away bulges as you work. When you are sure that the layers are firmly tacked, remove the pins and begin quilting.

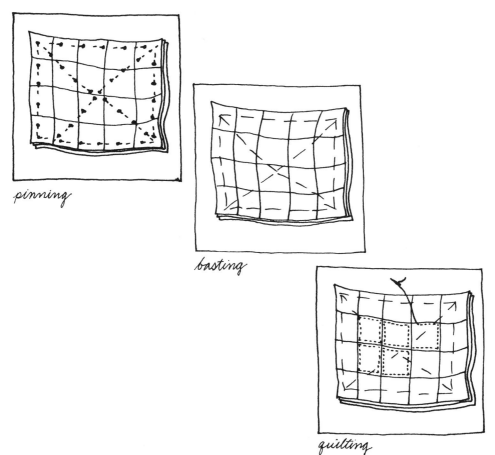

pinning

basting

quilting

Beginning to Stitch

To begin quilting, bring your needle, threaded with a single strand the length of your arm, up through the layers from back to front. When the thread is all the way through, give an **extra** tug on the knot, so that the knot will pull past the backing and lodge in the lining. It takes practice to learn how much pressure to apply. Fortunately, both the Basic Patchwork Quilted Pillow and the Log Cabin Name Bag projects keep the underside of the quilting hidden, so these are good pieces to practice with. Once the knot is in place, backstitch to secure it and continue quilting.

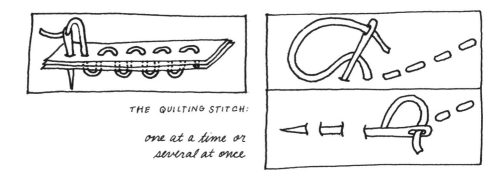

THE QUILTING STITCH:

one at a time or several at once

The Quilting Stitch

Traditionally quilting, or running, stitches are spaced every $\frac{1}{16}$ of an inch, but that kind of stitching takes practice. Do what's comfortable for you—trying to keep about five or six stitches showing on the quilt surface for every inch. When you become more comfortable with the materials, you may be able to make smaller stitches.

There are two methods for setting quilting stitches. The first is to make two separate strokes. Sending the needle up through the layers at right angles to the surface, receive it with your free hand and send it back down again on the same 90-degree angle. This is a reliable method. But, as you will soon discover, it's slow.

The second method, which is quicker, is to gather two or more stitches on your needle before you pull it through the fabric. This time, the stitch will begin and end on the top surface. Make sure you have caught all three layers for each stitch on the needle before you pull the needle all the way through. Be careful of shifting fabric with this latter method.

Special Tools

There are several sewing aids that can make a significant contribution to your quilting. The first is a thimble. It feels awkward at first, but as you start pushing the needle through the layers of a quilting project, you will appreciate the protective covering, and you will soon get used to the extra bulk. To make small quilting stitches use an in-between size 7–9 needle. Delicate and pointed, it should slip easily through the layers.

The next sewing helper is quilting thread. Strong and heavily waxed, it resists forming snags and knots and can endure a lot of hard tugging. Quilting thread is hard to find at local sewing supply counters, but it is available at specialty shops and through mail order catalogues. See the list on page 36.

The quilting frame is the last important sewing aid. Large, free-standing frames are available through the same sources as quilting thread, but they have drawbacks. They demand floor space, and, once they have been set up, they cannot be dismantled until the project has been completed. For economy of space, ease of stitching, and portability I prefer a quilting hoop. Available through the same sources, the hoop is easy to store away between quilting sessions. You can choose a free-standing model or one that you can hold on your lap. Although the quilting hoop is also wonderful for projects smaller than an actual quilt, very small areas may be quilted with an embroidery hoop, if the filling material is thin enough to fit into it.

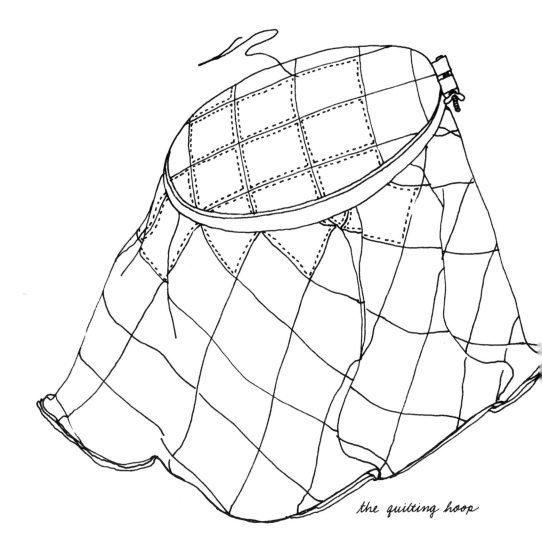

the quilting hoop

CRAZY QUILTING

Crazy quilting is a form of random patching in which pieces are overlapped to create a unified surface. By joining shapes of silk, velvet, ribbon, and lace to a backing material with extravagant embroidery stitches, you will invent a fantastic, magical vision.

Preparing Materials

Collect old neckties, pieces of velvet, satin, ribbon, and lace. Dismantle ties by opening up the back seam and discarding the interlining. Be sure, however, to save the silk linings and any interesting woven labels. Press creases out of all your materials before you begin to sew.

Backing Material

Backing material may be muslin or some other lightweight fabric, such as an old sheet, provided that it is strong and will be able to support several layers of material and stitching. Consider covering an old but simply cut article of clothing as Betsy did for the Crazy Quilt Skirt on page 142. If you are planning a crazy quilt bedcover, it is standard to prepare sixteen-inch-square blocks.

Placement

Begin by pinning a shape onto your base block or in a central location on the backing garment. All pieces are added right side up. Place the second piece so that at least one edge overlaps an edge of the fabric piece already in place. The edge remaining on top should be turned under with a ¼-inch hem. Additional patches may be laid down with their edges covering or slipped under an abutting piece. Edges that will eventually be covered by additional fabric should be left without a hem. Continue placing, turning under, and pinning until the entire surface is covered. The design choice is yours, provided that whatever edges are sitting on top in the final arrangement are tucked under with a ¼-inch hem. Although this technique is meant to have a random appearance, don't be afraid to change any fabric position as you are working to improve the design.

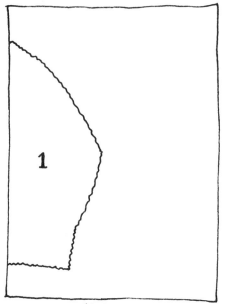

establish main piece

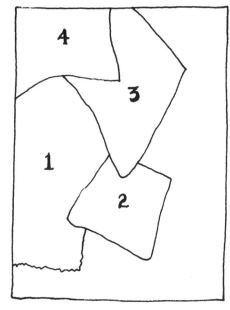

overlapping patches

CRAZY QUILTING

pinning in place

basting

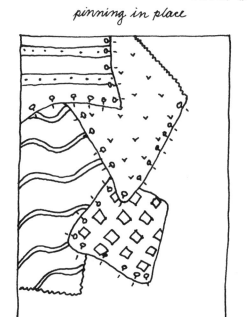

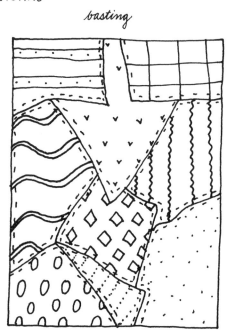

Basting

Thread your needle with a single strand of a color that will blend well with the patches. Bringing the needle and thread up from the wrong side, make running stitches that are short tacks on the surface and longer lengths on the back. This basting will become permanent when it is covered later by decorative embroidery. Baste all edges securely, remove the pins, and press.

Embroidery

All seams should be covered with decorative embroidery. You may choose to embroider with one stitch and carry it through the whole piece or you may work with various stitches throughout. The interior of the patches may also be filled with whimsical stitching.

CRAZY QUILTING

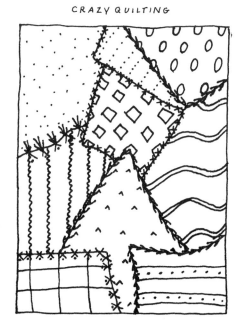

embroidery

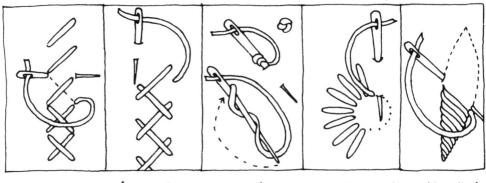

cross-stitch   herringbone   french knot   straight stitch   satin stitch
                stitch   or single satin
                                                    stitch

Backing and Tufting

If you have crazy-quilted a garment or a pillow top and the underside will be hidden when the article is in use, you will not need a lining. If, however, you have made a circle bag, a small item, or even a bedcover, you can make a lining by sewing a piece of fabric, cut to size, face to face with the crazy quilt cover. Do not close stitching, but leave an open space for reversing the object as you would a pillow. Turn right side out and topstitch ¼ inch from the edge. When making a bedcover you may join the two layers by "tufting." Thread a needle with doubled yarn or floss. Push the needle into a seam and through the backing, pulling until two inches are left on the surface for tying. Send the needle back to the surface ⅛ inch from the first stitch. Trim to a matching two inches. Using a square knot, tie all four strands together and trim to ½ inch. This tufting, which may be done with the knot on the right or wrong side of the bedcover, is also useful for joining together an appliqué or patchwork quilt top and backing. The tufting should be placed at regular intervals.

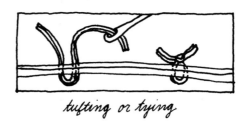

tufting or tying

CRAZY QUILT SKIRT (P.142)   CRAZY QUILT BAG (P.126)

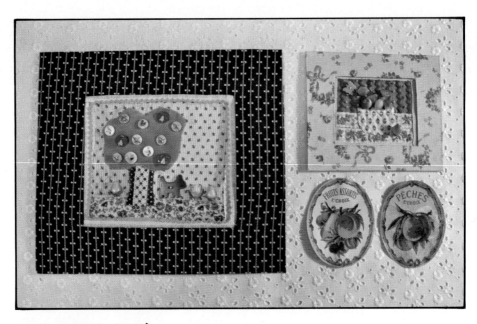

BUTTON PICTURES (P. 86)

THE APPLIQUÉ KITCHEN CATCHALL (P. 82)

APPLIQUÉ ALPHABET QUILT (P.90)   GINGHAM CAT (P.115)

WORK OVERALLS (top left P. 153)   OVERALL DRESS (top right P. 155)
COUNTRY BUTTERFLY DRESS (bottom left P. 135)   PATCHWORK KIMONO (bottom right P. 136)

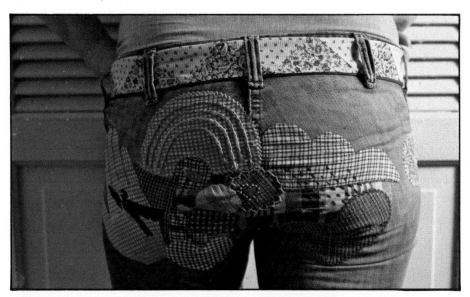

NICK'S JEANS (P.145)

DOLL WITH PARALLEL-STRIP-PATCHED DRESS AND HANDBAG (P.113)
TURTLE ORNAMENTS (P.105)   STRIP-PATCHED TURTLE (P.106)

PATCHWORK CAFÉ
CURTAINS (P. 81)

DIAGONAL RIBBON
PILLOW (P. 79)

THE APPLIQUÉ
STRAWBERRY
POUCH (P. 123)

BASIC PATCHWORK PILLOW (P. 65)   GINGHAM RIBBON PILLOW (P. 78)   PATCHWORK BEARS (P.107

JEAN JACKET (P. 151) PATCHWORK BELT (P. 133) APPLIQUÉ KNEE PATCHES (P. 148)

THE HOUSES-BY-THE-SEA APPLIQUÉ QUILT (P. 95)

PATCHWORK SUPERSHIRT (P. 140) MELANIE'S DELICATE PATCHWORK PANTS (P. 138) SUMMER PARALLEL-STRIP-PATCH BAG (P. 120)

ANIMAL APPLIQUÉ CLOTHES FOR CHILDREN (P. 139)   LOG CABIN NAME BAG (P. 129)

PATCHWORK TABLECLOTH (P.102)   EASY APPLIQUÉ SATCHEL (P.118)

6

The Projects:
A Matter for Interpretation

THE BASIC PATCHWORK QUILTED PILLOW

How to Make a Patchwork Top,
How to Quilt It,
How to Make a Basic Pillow Form

This pillow is an ideal introduction to patchwork and quilting. Lap-sized and manageable, it can be as city-sophisticated or as country-charming as the fabrics you choose. It will also help you to discover many of the pleasures and iron out the pitfalls of patchwork in one evening.

The instructions for making the patchwork pillow top are extremely detailed because the procedure is exactly the same for making a larger pieced quilt. The pillow construction described is also basic to many other patchwork projects. Try completing this pillow first if you intend eventually to make a sprawling, challenging quilt.

If this is your first sewing experience, I recommend completing the patched, quilted pillow top by hand. Although machine sewing is certainly faster, you will have more control of your patches if you hand-stitch. You will attain the delicacy of hand quilting that has never been rivaled by the rigid, impersonal machine. Use the machine, which is strong, to assemble the pillow once the patchwork and quilting is complete.

THE BASIC PATCHWORK PILLOW: *quilting is indicated by dotted lines*

Materials for the
Basic Patchwork Quilted Pillow

All measurements are given in finished sizes. Be sure to allow ¼ inch for seam allowances on every measurement specified below when you are cutting. The completed pillow is 17 inches by 17 inches.

Fabric

16 3″ × 3″ squares	Choose at least 2 different fabric patterns to be alternated when the squares are sewn in position, as shown in the drawing of the Basic Patchwork Quilted Pillow.
36 3″ × 2″ × 2″ triangles	Choose 2 more pattern motifs. Cut 16 triangles of one pattern and 20 of the other.

4 outside strips
  2 measuring 4¼″ × 14″
  2 measuring 4½″ × 17″
	All of a fifth fabric.

1 pillow backing 17″ × 17″	The fifth fabric again.
1 quilt backing 17″ × 17″	To be made from an old sheet or some other soft cotton scrap material. It will not show in the finished pillow because it will be covered by stuffing and pillow backing. Were this an actual quilt, however, it *would* show and you should choose an appropriate fabric.
1 quilt interlining 17″ × 17″	Soft, preshrunk flannel or polyester quilt batting sold in precut quilt-sized sheets.
sewing thread	For ease in stitching the patchwork increments, use bel-waxed thread which can be found easily at sewing supply counters. Cotton or polyester are also acceptable. For quilting the

pillow top, special quilting thread, if available (see page 36), is terrific. Basting thread is handy for temporary stitching.

sewing needle

Use a size 7–9 needle. It may seem small at first, but it's great for in and out quilt stitchery.

scissors

If they are sharp, they will be a great help. If they are dull, they will be an awful hindrance. They should have at least 4″ straight blades.

pillow stuffing

Dacron Fiberfil, available in bags at sewing supply stores and the five-and-ten, handles easily, is nonallergenic, and gives a flexible, fluffy shape to the pillow. Scraps of fabric cut into small pieces and old, cut-up panty hose are acceptable. I don't recommend foam fillings. Aside from their stubborn, rocklike form, they tend to become soggy.

shirt cardboard and several 3″ × 5″ index cards

For the templates.

ruler
medium pencil or tailor's chalk

In colors contrasting to the fabric.

X-Acto knife

For cutting out templates.

iron

For keeping patchwork pieces in shape.

Procedure

The template   I used 3″ × 5″ index cards, ruler, pencil, and X-Acto knife to make the templates for this pillow. With three sides of the square already established, the fourth is found easily by measuring in three inches from the edge. Make sure to do it in at least three places for accuracy. The triangle was made by dividing the three-inch square in half diagonally and then in half again so the long side of the remaining triangle is three inches. To get accurate sides and edges, use a ruler, pencil, and X-Acto to mark and cut. The strips were also measured with a ruler and pencil and were cut from shirt cardboard.

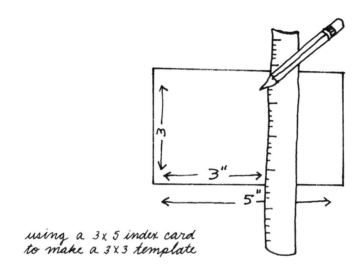

using a 3 x 5 index card
to make a 3 x 3 template

The plan   Chart your color placement on paper before you begin marking and cutting so you will be sure to have the correct number of squares, triangles, and strips in the right colors. You may also refer to the drawing of the Basic Patchwork Quilted Pillow on page 66. Keep your layout nearby when you work for easy reference.

Preliminary pressing   Get your iron out now and give all of your fabric a preliminary pressing on the wrong side. Keep the iron handy, because you will be needing it again soon.

Marking and cutting the squares   Lay your fabric on a flat, hard surface, wrong side up. Check your chart to see how many squares you need of the color you are working on. Then, securing the template with one hand, carefully trace around its shape with a medium pencil or chalk. This will be your sewing line. Make sure the template sits on the fabric so one edge runs parallel to the grain. This will prevent puckering and pulling later. Move the template over and continue tracing squares, allowing at least ½-inch between each two shapes (¼-inch for each square). When you have finished tracing off the specified amount, carefully cut around each square, leaving the ¼-inch margin on all sides. Stack your pieces and mark them off on your chart. Continue marking, cutting, stacking, and checking until all of your squares, triangles, and strips are prepared.

Placement   Lay out all of your cut pieces in the correct arrangement, right side up, in front of you. They will cover an area significantly larger than the finished pillow because the extra ¼-inch seam allowances have not yet been used.

Pinning to register   Pinning is a time-consuming but necessary precaution in making accurately registered patchwork. The procedure I am about to describe has two steps.

Since you will begin your sewing in the area composed of squares, choose two contrasting squares sitting side by side in your layout. Flip one over the other so they are sitting face to face.

PINNING TO REGISTER

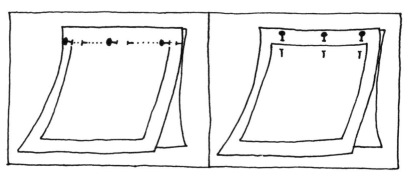

step one: aligning the squares   step two: final pinning

Step one—aligning the squares Align the squares by placing three pins into the sewing line. If you push a pin through one end of the line, it should meet the sewing line of the facing piece in exactly the same place. Repeat the process at the other end of the line and then in the middle. If the lines don't match up, correct the placement using the pin method to locate the right position. Be exacting now and you will be glad later. Every increment that a square is off register will be multiplied as you join the other pieces.

Step two—final pinning The first pinning was necessary to align the patches, but the pins must be replaced to make room for the stitching. Look at the drawing and place three pins at right angles to the sewing line when you are satisfied that the pieces are correctly aligned. *Remove the first three pins only after you have placed the second three in position* to retain the registration.

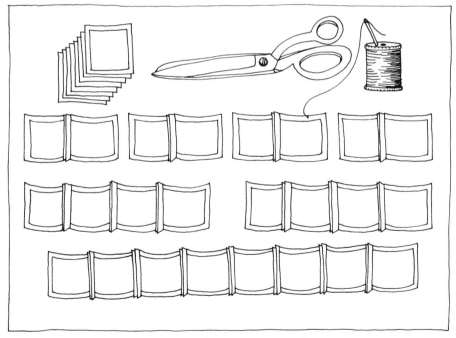

PATCHWORK: *joining pairs to build a strip*

Sewing Once you have accurately registered your first two patches, you are ready to sew. Knot your thread and bring it up through the exact beginning of the sewing line. Make a small running stitch, as shown on page 49, and then one backstitch to secure the thread. Then continue to make running stitches along the line until you reach the end. Backstitch once again to secure the thread and bring the needle up for the final time through the exact end of the line. Knot securely and cut off needle and extra thread. Remove the registration pins. Continue to sew adjoining squares in units of two, putting each pair back in your layout when it is sewn. This will enable you to keep track of them and they will be ready for the next procedure.

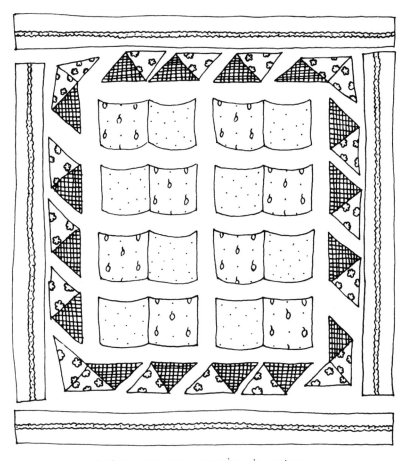

BASIC LAYOUT: *sewing in pairs*

Pressing   After all of your squares have been sewn into units of two and the pins have been removed, gently press them. Apply steam on the wrong side of the fabric, pressing seam allowances to one side. Although machine stitching is generally pressed with the seams open, this technique puts unnecessary strain on the hand stitching. The idea of pressing is to get the patches to lie flat, but not to reveal the stitching. Especially with hand work, if the stitches are showing, there is too much pull on them.

Continue sewing by pinning and joining pairs (pairs are now sewn units of two) until all four cross strips have been completed. Press them open.

Final sewing of the central unit   Once all of the strips have been completed, place two strips right sides together. Refer to your layout to determine which edges to sew together. Sew, using the same running stitch technique, and again, sew in pairs. This time, however, each single unit is a strip. When the central block of squares has been totally assembled and pressed, you are ready to begin working with triangles.

Sewing triangles   You will use the same method of sewing pairs into strips when you work with triangles, but watch out to sew the correct sides together. It can be tricky. This is an especially good time to have all of your pieces laid out in front of you. Flip a triangle over its neighbor to see what a funny position they are in when being sewn. Remember, you will always be sewing short sides together, although the triangles will appear to be on a strange angle when pinned face to face. Sew the triangles into four strips of nine. The strips will actually be two staggered rows because of the triangular shapes. Join the shorter side of a strip to each outside edge of the block of squares, adding the extra triangles where they are needed to complete the corners. When the corners are sewn (same running stitch, of course), you are ready to add the final outside pieces.

Sew the 14-inch strips on first. Add the 17-inch ones and sew right into the 14-inch ones at each end. Press open.

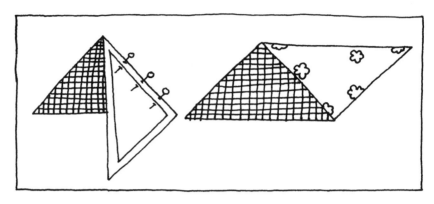

sewing triangles

Quilting

Assembling the materials   When your patchwork top has been given a final pressing, you are ready to begin quilting. For this you will need quilt interlining, backing fabric, needle, thread (quilting thread will make the job easier, and basting thread is also useful), ruler, pencil or chalk, and your pieced top.

Placement of the layers   On a flat, hard surface, make a sandwich by laying out the quilt backing (since it won't show in the finished pillow, it doesn't matter which side is out), the quilt interlining, and the patchwork top, right side up. You are about to make a quilted top by joining the three layers together in actual position. The quilt stitching will be permanent. The actual pillow will be assembled later in a different process, by sewing on a pillow back. To make sure your assemblage is correct, refer to the drawing on page 55. Make sure the interlining and the backing have at least a ¼-inch seam allowance all around.

Basting the layers   Once the sandwich is assembled, sitting flat without any bulges, you may baste. If, in the beginning, you find that you have too much layer shifting, you will have to pin them together even before you baste. Basting is another of those safety measures to prevent anxiety later. Start from the center of the piece and with medium to large running stitches, work out diagonally to the corners in a straight line. Smooth the fabric as you go to prevent buckling. Knot and end off. Return to the center and work outward again to the next empty corner. Continue to ease the fabric flat as you go. When all the diagonals have been sewn, baste around the outside edge.

Quilting the layers   Quilting is done with tiny running stitches as shown on page 58. As with basting, it is worked from the center of the piece outward. This time, however, the stitches are small, evenly spaced, and are meant to hold permanently. As you set your quilting stitches, your basting will become obsolete. If it gets in the way of your work, remove it as you go. If it is not interfering, wait until the quilting has been completed before you remove it.

The quilting stitches on this pillow were made diagonally through the squares radiating from a central circle. The stitching is also placed just inside the outer edges of the four middle squares and just inside the outer edge of the first row of triangles. The pattern is indicated by a dotted line in the drawing of the completed Basic Patchwork Quilted Pillow on page 66. Use it as a guide or invent your own placement. Always remember to work from the center of the bulk outward to prevent unwanted shifting. For extra quilting hints, read the section on quilting which begins on page 54.

Making the Pillow

To make the pillow, we return to the technique of sewing face to face and then turning inside out. Press the pillow backing fabric and rule out a 17-inch square on the wrong side. Cut out and leave the standard ¼-inch seam allowance on all sides. Place the quilted pillow top (never, by the way, press anything quilted) face to face with the pillow back. Make sure the outside border of the top is registered with the backing material. Pin around the edges at right angles to the sewing line. If you have a sewing machine, this is a good time to use it. If not, firmly hand-stitch around the outside sewing edge of the pillow. Leave about a five-inch opening for reversing the pillow and putting in the stuffing. For strength, it is wise to include the four corners of the pillow in the original stitching, leaving the hole for reversing and stuffing in the middle of one of the sides (as shown in the pillow-construction diagram). When the sewing is done, snip the corners on a diagonal, close to but not through the stitching. This will allow the corners to take form. Reverse the pillow by pulling the inside through the open hole. Poke the corners out with a crochet hook or the blunt end of a pencil. Stuff the Dacron Fiberfil (or whatever you have chosen for stuffing material) through the opening, using the same long instrument to help distribute the filling evenly. When the pillow has

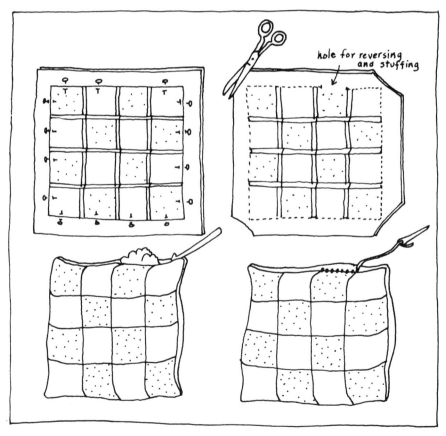

basic pillow construction

become a gentle, fluffy form, push the seam allowance into the hole, making the side smooth. Sew up the gap with tiny hand stitches.

THE RIBBON PILLOWS

Betsy and I had an exhilarating time collecting ribbons for these pillows in a neighborhood trim shop. Overwhelmed, at first, by the infinite possibilities in front of us, we chose several absolute favorites as color keys and then selected only ribbons that would fit into our scheme. It meant leaving a lot of beauties behind, but it also meant having exciting combinations to work with when we got home.

gingham ribbon pillow

Gingham Ribbon Pillow

Cut two pieces of gingham in the pillow size you want. Be sure to leave a seam allowance. With gingham you can let the position of the checks guide you. Cut ribbons and rickrack to the same lengths as your pillow. Lay them on the right side of the front panel. Place these decorations in one direction only, either horizontally or vertically. Pin the ribbons in place. Use a few dabs of fabric glue to tack rickrack in position because it tends to elude pins.

Stitch ribbons along each edge with a blending color of thread and sew rickrack down the middle. If you use a sewing machine, use a medium-length machine straight stitch. If you intend to machine stitch in several colors (if the outside edges of the ribbons change radically from ribbon to ribbon), change only the needle thread, because the bobbin stitching will not show on the finished pillow. This is a big time saver.

If you are working by hand, use a blindstitch to attach the ribbons and a running stitch through the center to fasten the rickrack.

step one: stitching down ribbons running in the same direction

Place and pin the ribbons and trims that run in the other direction and stitch them in place.

Finish the pillow according to the directions in the basic pillow assembly section on page 75. Stitch ¼ inch in from all edges.

Diagonal Ribbon Pillow

Cut two pieces of fabric 13½" × 13½". The top base piece will not show in the finished pillow, so use muslin or some other inexpensive, sturdy fabric. Use velvet, velveteen, or any other appropriate material for the back. You will also need an assortment of carefully chosen, color-coordinated ribbons in half-yard lengths, which you will be sewing to the muslin. Only the central ribbon will take up the full eighteen inches that you have allowed but any pieces that are left can be used later as appliqués or patch material.

Experiment with the arrangement of the ribbons. When you are pleased with the order, take the center diagonal ribbon and pin it in place on the muslin. Stitch down each edge with a blending color of thread. Next, pin the two ribbons that sit on either

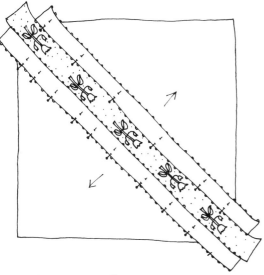

working from the center outward

adding a ruffle

side of the central strip to the muslin. Each new addition should abut the one next to it without concealing any edges or revealing any muslin. Continue sewing down ribbon strips until the entire square is covered.

Finish the pillow according to the basic instructions given on page 75.

If you want to add a ruffle, do it while you are constructing the pillow. Baste a length of eyelet lace to the face of the pillow panel around the outside circumference, easing it gently around the corners. The outer, or decorative, edge of the ruffle should be facing toward the center of the pillow as shown in the diagram. The ruffle edge to be attached to the pillow body should stick out slightly between the two layers to ensure that it will be caught in the final stitching. If you have placed and pinned the eyelet correctly, the scalloped ruffled edge will be free when you reverse the pillow.

diagonal ribbon pillow

patchwork café curtains

PATCHWORK CAFÉ CURTAINS

Create a spectacular window arrangement by patching together some favorite pieces of cotton. The central red panels of the patchwork curtains are practically family heirlooms. Stored away in a trunk for forty years, the flowered calico once hung in my family's summer cottage. The pieces seemed at first to be too small for my own window, but I was determined to make them fit. Searching through fabric outlets and department stores, I finally unearthed some new patterned material that was compatible in both feeling and color to my 1930s print. Patching the new additions to the old gave my treasured curtains new life.

You can make your own wonderful curtains with some favorite fabric and a yardstick. The important measurement is the window width. Cheery, soft-looking curtains should actually be twice the width of the area that they cover. Construct these curtains as you would any other patchwork project and build the panels to your own specifications. Leave extra seam allowance of at least three inches along the top edge, fold it over toward the back, and stitch two parallel lines across the top at least one inch down. Since this will be the tunnel for the curtain rod, experiment first to determine the necessary width of the tunnel. Make sure you are fairly accurate. If the tunnel is too small, the rod won't fit through, and if it's too wide the curtains will fall limply. Hang the curtains in place and pin the hem in position. Remove the curtains to sew the hem. Press and hang again. Distribute the folds evenly and tie back each side gracefully with ribbons, which are anchored to the wall with thumbtacks.

THE APPLIQUÉ KITCHEN CATCHALL

The appliqué kitchen hanging is a handy pocket organizer on the wall for utensils. Completely washable and stitched by machine, it provides a bonus storage area and welcome good cheer for a neglected kitchen.

Cut and hem the 22″ × 32″ denim base first. Then cut the 6½″ × 30″ checkered tablecloth. Pin under the edges of the tablecloth, press, and appliqué to the denim base with a straight stitch.

To build the pocketed unit, cut a 14¾″ × 17½″ flowered fabric base and nine 3¼-inch-square contrasting pockets. Fold back the top edge of each pocket ¼ inch and pin ribbon along the top. Stitch along both edges of the ribbon. Fold under and pin the other three sides of the pockets. Pin the pockets in position on the flowered base and stitch down.

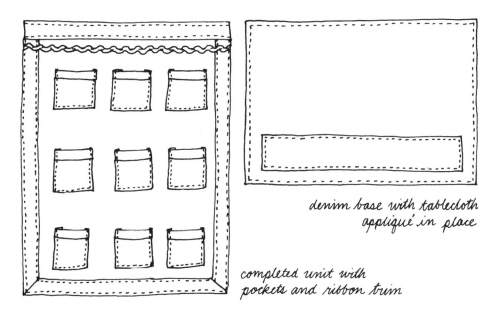

denim base with tablecloth
appliqué in place

completed unit with
pockets and ribbon trim

Fold the outer hem of the completed pocketed panel under and pin the entire unit in place on the tablecloth area.

Pin a length of ribbon or ribbons as shown in the drawing around the perimeter of the pocketed panel, folding the corners neatly. Stitch both edges of the ribbon border to the denim base.

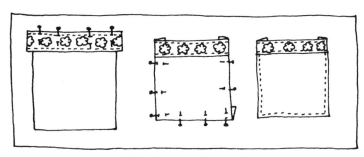

BUILDING A POCKET:

1. pinning the ribbon along the top
2. folding under and pinning the other three sides
3. topstitching the three sides

For extra strength, stitch a line ⅛ inch around the outside of each pocket, on the denim base, being careful not to sew into the pockets, and especially not into the open pocket tops.

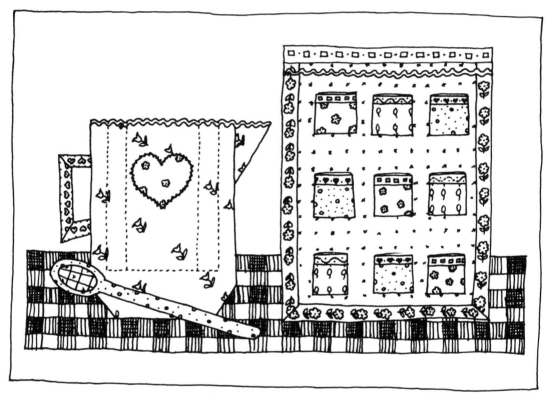

the appliqué kitchen catchall

Construct the pitcher next. It is approximately 9½″ × 11½″ with a small triangular spout. Cut a heart-shaped decoration to the sewing line and zigzag it to the front of the pitcher. Pin the spout in place and baste under the top hem of both pitcher and spout. With a few dabs of fabric glue tack the rickrack along the basted top edge and stitch it down. Fold under all other edges of the pitcher and pin in position on the tablecloth next to the pocketed unit. Pin on a ribbon handle, with the corners folded on the diagonal abutting the pitcher, so the ribbon ends are hidden. Stitch around the outside edge of the pitcher, then the spout, and then the handle. Make sure to leave the top of the pitcher and spout open.

Delineate a pocket and four tunnels for cooking utensils by stitching three sides of a rectangle into the pitcher. Again, the top edge will be left open. Stitch 9 inches down the side of the pitcher, 7 inches across, and 9 inches up again. Leave about 1¼ inches between the outside edge of the pitcher and the vertical stitch lines. Working toward the center of the pitcher, stitch two more verticals with 1¼ inches between them.

As a final decoration, cut, baste, pin in position, and machine appliqué a spoon just below the pitcher. Give the bowl of the spoon some depth with an oval of contrasting fabric. Be sure the spoon is placed well below the stitched pockets in the pitcher.

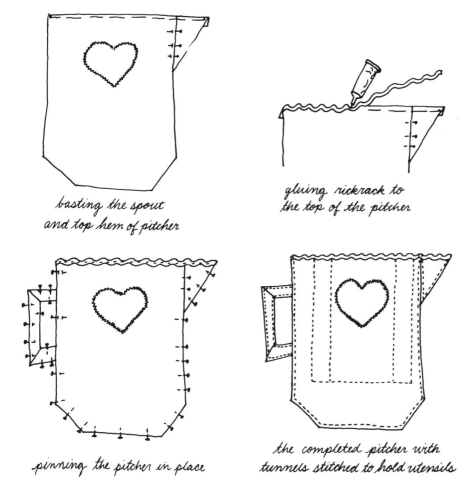

basting the spout
and top hem of pitcher

gluing rickrack to
the top of the pitcher

pinning the pitcher in place

the completed pitcher with
tunnels stitched to hold utensils

BUTTON PICTURES

Stitch your favorite buttons into a patchwork, appliqué environment that will enhance their delicacy and charm.

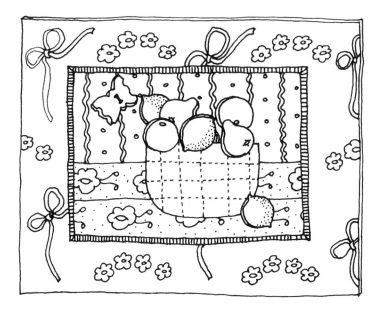

the fruit bowl

The Button Fruit Bowl Picture

The fruit bowl rests on a base of mustard-color velvet. All stitching was done by hand. The rickrack and bead wallpaper was stitched in place first, and then the tablecloth—two strips of ribbon—was appliquéd in the foreground. The bowl shape was applied on top with quilting stitches for added texture. The fruit buttons and butterfly were then sewn down. Flower- or vegetable-shaped buttons would work just as well.

The entire scene was framed with an inner ring of grosgrain and an outer mat of carefully chosen printed cotton. In order to add this decorative frame, you will have to back the button scene

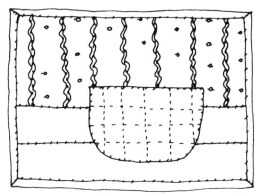

completed appliqué picture ready for buttons

with cardboard. Add the grosgrain to the edges of the picture first, leaving an extra ½-inch of the velvet fabric beyond the ribbon on all sides. With an X-Acto knife cut the cardboard to the picture measurement just up to the outer edge of the ribbon. Clip the corners of the button picture on the diagonal so they will fold neatly around the cardboard.

Turn the picture face down and cover the exposed area with spray adhesive. Be sure that you read the instructions on the label of the can and that the work space is well protected and well ventilated. Place the cardboard on the now-sticky back of the button picture and press. Turn the cardboard so the picture faces front. Gently smooth out any surface bubbles. Wrap the fabric allowance around the edge of the cardboard and press down with your hand.

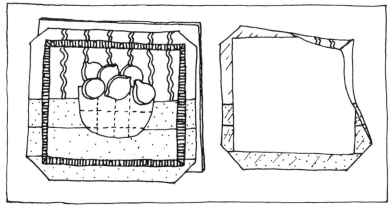

backing the button picture with cardboard

Decide what size you want for the outer frame and cut it out of matboard to size. Make sure the inside opening of the mat is a tiny bit smaller than the actual picture so the picture won't fall through.

Cut a corresponding shape of fabric with at least a ¾-inch seam allowance on the inside and outside of the shape.

Place the fabric frame face down and hold the cardboard mat firmly on top. For clean folding, make diagonal slices in each outside corner in the same way you snipped the corners of the fabric scene. Also make diagonal slashes in the inner corners of the fabric just up to the cardboard so the fabric will be able to wrap easily.

Temporarily remove the cardboard frame and cover the wrong side of the fabric frame (it should already be in correct position with the wrong side up) with spray adhesive. Hold the cardboard mat over the sprayed material and lower it carefully into place. Press down and wrap the inner seam allowance around the inside edge of the cardboard, smoothing it evenly with your fingers. Press the cardboard with the side of your fist to make sure the frame and fabric are joining.

Wrap the outer fabric allowance around the cardboard. Turn the mat right side up and push out any air pockets with the long side of a ruler. Center the picture in the mat and use masking tape on the back to fix the picture in position. Use gummed picture hooks to hang.

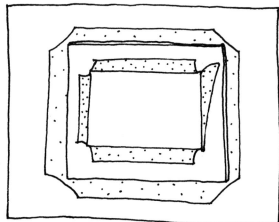

*covering a cardboard mat
with fabric
shown from the back*

the button tree picture

The Button Tree Picture

Use the same principles to construct and frame the Button Tree Picture that are described in the instructions for the Button Fruit Bowl Picture.

Patch together two different cotton fabrics to make the sky and the ground plane. Make the trunk by stitching ribbon down the center of a strip of fabric. The treetop is velvet. Appliqué the trunk and treetop in place. When the appliqué is complete, turn the picture face down and gently slice a small opening into the trunk and treetop areas, so they can be stuffed. Be careful to pierce only the backing. Push in a tiny bit of stuffing with the aid of a pencil or crochet hook and stitch up the holes. Turn the picture face up again and sew on the decorative buttons. In this case I used a dog, tulips, fruit, and birds, but you may have found different ones.

Mount the button picture on cardboard as described in the directions for the fruit bowl. Trim the edges with ribbon and rickrack. The outside mat is made according to the directions given in the fruit bowl section.

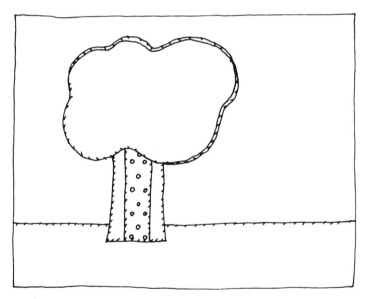

the completed appliqué picture ready for buttons

THE APPLIQUÉ ALPHABET QUILT

The appliqué alphabet quilt is a spectacular gift for your favorite baby. Betsy Potter's quilt has an alphabet theme, but animals, flowers, or any other whimsical motif could also work beautifully. The secret ingredient in this project is variety. Embroidery, beads, buttons, lace, ribbon, rickrack, and carefully coordinated printed fabrics have been stitched together for visual texture and surprise.

the appliqué alphabet quilt

Cut twenty-eight 5-inch squares out of solid-color fabrics for the appliqué background pieces. They will eventually be applied four across and seven down to a larger backing material measuring 26″ × 44″. Decide how you will place your background squares and make note of your decision on a piece of paper for reference later.

Complete each individual appliqué square according to the directions starting on page 44. Use the same images that Betsy chose—with a child's name in the first square and date of birth in the last—or invent your own themes and designs.

Betsy's quilt was sewn by hand, almost entirely with the running stitch. Areas that were particularly hard to control, like the apple's stem and the yak's head, were made with iron-on tape. You may, however, decide to use other types of hand stitches or even the sewing machine.

When the appliqué squares are completed, turn under the edges and baste each square in position face up on the large background piece according to your plan. Try to line up vertical and horizontal edges as much as possible. You may find that you cannot do this exactly; slight unevenness is unavoidable. If you are using a checked or gingham background, as Betsy did, you can line up your squares with the pattern of the backing fabric.

Quilting

When all the squares are basted down, lay out the appliqué top, face down on a flat surface. Since the fabric must be absolutely flat, try taping the edges of the appliqué top to the work surface. This should prevent buckling or shifting. Lay out the batting or quilt filling in position over the appliqué top and baste it into place. On top of that, place the backing sheet face up, and baste the three layers together.

Pick up the basted quilt sandwich and quilt around each square to fasten the three layers. Also consider quilting around each major shape in each square and down the long passages between the squares.

When you have finished quilting, bind the edges with seam binding or contrasting fabric, and miter the corners as shown. Sew plastic curtain rings, from the five-and-ten-cent store, across the top of the back if you want to hang the quilt.

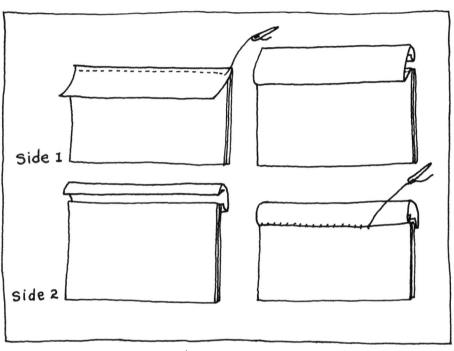

binding edges

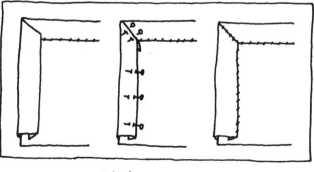

mitering corners

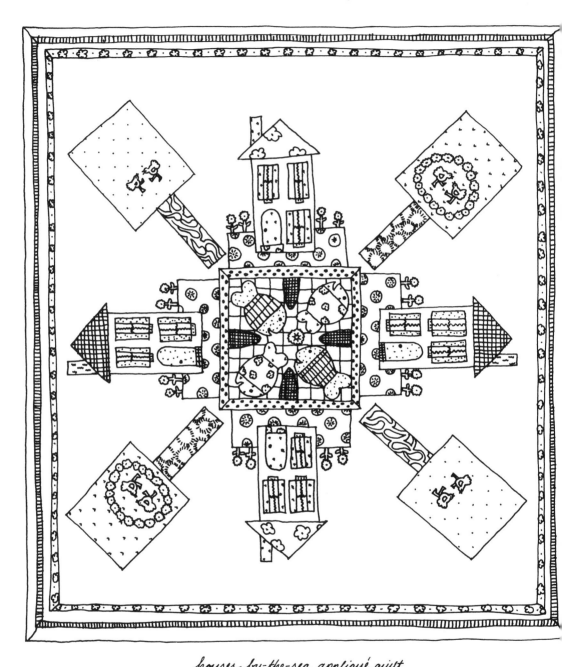

houses-by-the-sea appliqué quilt

THE HOUSES-BY-THE-SEA APPLIQUÉ QUILT

The Houses-by-the-Sea Appliqué Quilt is a cheerful, very off-beat bedcover. The appliqué top is made almost entirely with the zigzag stitching of a sewing machine except for a few touches of handwork such as the Yo-Yo flowers. Because of its overwhelming size, I recommend it for experienced zigzaggers.

The appliqué top and the backing sheet are both standard 81" × 104" full flat percale sheets. I recommend buying two good-quality sheets of the same brand for this project. Hoping to save money, I originally tried to use a poorer quality of sheet for the backing. When I began to assemble the quilt, I discovered that the undersheeting was so lopsided that I would have to cut the appliqué top if I wanted it to match the bottom. Naturally, I decided to reinvest in a sheet with the same proportions as the top. Also make sure, as I did, when buying a sheet for this project, that there is no decorative ruffle along the top edge. The ruffle, unless completely incorporated into the appliqué design, will make it hard for the sheet to transform successfully from "sheet" to "quilt."

The sheet you are working on is large, so clear away a roomy space around your sewing machine. Because of its size, the sheet is bound to become unwieldy as you stitch. Check occasionally to make sure you are sewing only what you intend to. Stop when you get to corners of the appliqué shapes to reestablish any control you might have lost. Make sure your stitches are almost 100 per cent inside the appliqué shape.

First, complete the central area of fish on a gingham sea measuring 18½ inches square. You can create two-tone fish by laying middle sections over fish bodies as shown. Use two different fabric combinations. The fish—with the middle sections pinned over them—should be pinned to the background with two swimming toward each other and two swimming away. Space four leaf shapes evenly between each two fish. When all shapes are pinned, appliqué with a zigzag stitch.

Establish the center of the quilt by folding the quilt horizontally and then vertically. Press gently and unfold. Put long

zigzag a middle section over the fish bodies to make two-tone fish

running stitches in the creases. Then, using the basting to guide you, pin the fish square in the center of the appliqué top. Pin grosgrain ribbon around the perimeter of the appliquéd fish square to cover the edges. Machine straight stitch along both edges of the ribbon. This will appliqué the sea in place.

Next, cut out four 12″ × 14″ shapes for the houses. Build zig-zag doors, front steps, windows, and rickrack divisions, shutters, roofs, and chimneys. The ribbon windowsills should be pinned with cut edges turned under and then straight stitched.

When the houses are assembled, cut four matching rectangular ground planes. Pin the ground planes in place on each side of the central fish area so they abut the ribbon. Then center and

placing the central panel

pin the houses to the ground planes and appliqué everything in position. Zigzag around each house first, beginning at the bottom edge. Include the roof and the chimney. Then stitch the ground plane.

Make Yo-Yos next according to directions on page 100. Then plant the garden by hand-stitching two Yo-Yo flowers on each side of each house with six-strand green embroidery floss. With green and lavender, cross-stitch in the center of each flower until you have made a sunburst design. Delineate the flower stems and leaves with the same green floss, using a running stitch. Cut a template in the stem and leaf shape and lightly trace it in position as a guide.

zig zag appliqué house on ground plane

Pin bird shapes, wings, legs, and beaks to the treetop rectangles and appliqué in the same way you trimmed the houses. Pin the tree trunks and tops in place on the quilt top and zigzag in place.

Run a long thread through a line of about nineteen Yo-Yos to establish a chain. Pin the chain in place around the birds on two of the trees. Appliqué them in position with a hemstitch.

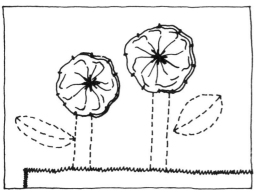

yo-yo flowers with quilted stems

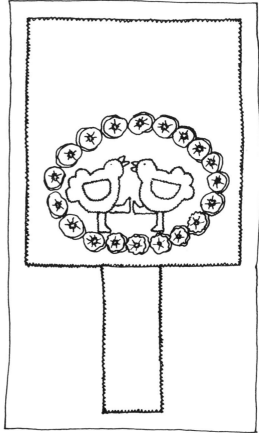

tree with birds and yo-yos

Also appliqué a Yo-Yo in the middle of the swimming-fish square. Sew on lightweight buttons for the fish eyes.

To put on the final trim you will need ten yards each of two different ribbons. I recommend one thin strand of grosgrain and one row of flowered cotton. Put the inner row 4 inches from the edge of the sheet and the outer row 3 inches from the edge. Pin them in position, making sure that the corners are folded neatly. Attach with a machine straight stitch.

The lining is one sheet of Dacron batting, which comes slightly larger than the appliqué top. I used the batting straight from the roll for extra thickness. If you want a thinner, lighter, more manageable cover, use cotton flannel.

I tried completing my quilt with hand stitches, but I don't recommend it because the layers of sheeting are so thick. Instead I recommend tufting as described on page 64.

To finish the edges, carefully cut away an inch of appliqué top and lining on all sides. Fold the bottom layer around the upper layers, fold under to form a hem, and blindstitch. Make sure to miter the corners.

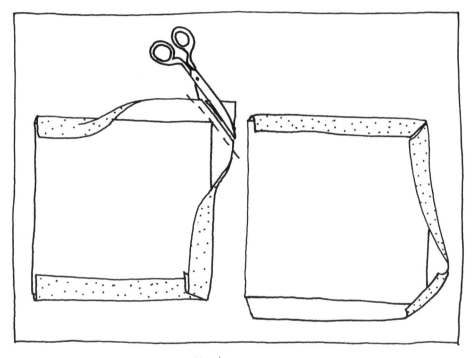

mitering corners

YO-YOS

Yo-Yos are whimsical, decorative flower forms. Made from circular patches, they are hemmed and gathered into small rosettes. Yo-Yos are used as flowers in the garden in the Houses-by-the-Sea Appliqué Quilt, but they can also be used to build a bed-

YO-YOS: cut circle, turn under hem with running stitch and draw into position

cover or garment or as trim on any piece of needlework. Stitch them to each other or appliqué them to a base fabric.

To make a Yo-Yo, draw a circle at least twice the size of the finished flowerlet onto cardboard and cut it out. Large tin cans make terrific ready-to-use templates. Trace the circular shape onto the wrong side of the fabric. The Yo-Yos for the Houses-by-the-Sea Quilt measure 3¼ inches across before being hemmed and drawn into position. Cut out the fabric ¼ inch from the line. Turn in the edges of the circular piece right up to the line. Make sure the hem falls over the wrong side of the fabric. Using a short running stitch, sew into the seam allowance ⅛ inch from the edge, all the way around. Your stitching must be continuous, with no backstitches. The Yo-Yo is formed when you pull on the thread, forcing the edges of the circle to pull together and leaving a hole in the middle. Since the thread will have to support the tension of the fabric, use quilting thread or regular sewing thread doubled. When you begin stitching, bring your needle up from the underside so the knot will be hidden when the Yo-Yo is used. Stitch evenly around the perimeter and then pull smoothly to pull the circle into a Yo-Yo. Arrange the folds evenly and fasten with a few backstitches. Flatten the Yo-Yo and press with a damp cloth and warm iron.

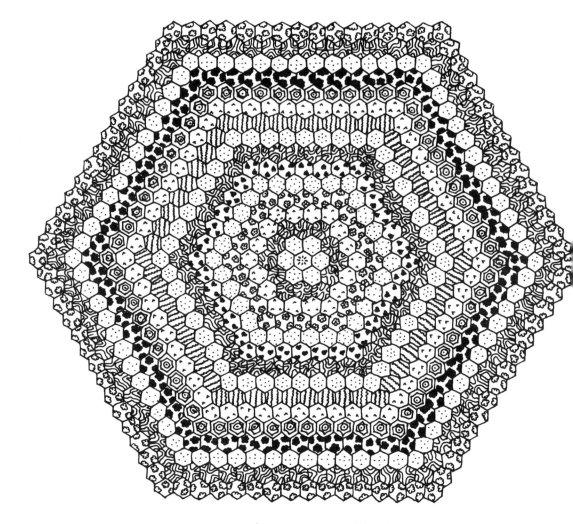

the patchwork tablecloth

THE PATCHWORK TABLECLOTH

Betsy's color-soaked tablecloth is bursting with energy. Made of concentric rings of hexagons, the overall shape of the cloth is, of course, six-sided. When you are choosing materials for a cloth of your own, look for small prints and solids. A half-yard should be enough for a concentric ring.

Accuracy is particularly important in this project, so use a compass to devise your hexagon template. With the compass draw a circle with the diameter the size you want for the finished hexagon. Betsy's hexagons measure 2 ¾ inches across. Place the compass so the pencil point rests on the exact middle of the circle and the needle point rests exactly on the circle's circumference. Swing the pencil point from the middle so it intersects the circumference with a line. Place the compass point on this intersection and repeat the swing until a second intersection has been marked. Move the compass point to this second marking and swing the compass to locate a third intersection. Continue around the circle until there are six evenly spaced intersections marked. To make a perfect hexagon, connect the points with a pencil and ruler. If you are planning to make Betsy's tablecloth, be sure to draw your hexagon template on a heavy cardboard so the edges don't wear out. Sand away any roughness, or make several templates out of lighter-weight cardboard as replacements.

Lay out and trace your template on the wrong side of the fabric as described in the patchwork section on page 42. Cut one hexagon for the center, six for the second ring, twelve for the third, eighteen for the fourth, etc. Each successive ring has six more than the previous one.

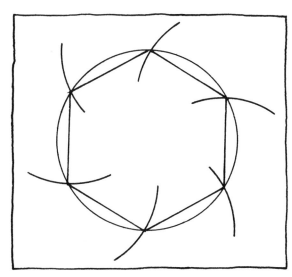

constructing a hexagon

Begin by sewing one hexagon of ring one to the middle hexagon on one edge only. Follow all rules concerning patchwork (turn to page 39). Each new addition in ring one will be joined in two places—to the hexagon in the center and to the hexagon right next to it. You will have to ease each piece into position. Follow the chart until you finish the ring.

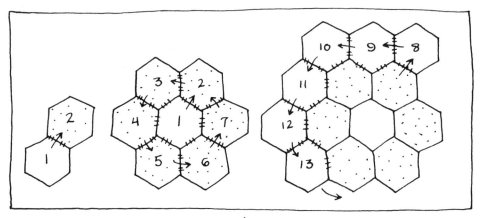

joining hexagons

Begin the next ring in a new color. The first new hexagon in each new ring will be attached to the preceding ring in one place only. The second hexagon will be attached in three places, the third in two places, and the fourth in three places again. The number of sides to be attached is determined by the preceding ring. Corner attachments require two seams. Interior attachments need three. Study the diagram to understand why this happens. There are, however, other order choices you can make when affixing hexagons, if you prefer. It will be easier to control your hexagons if you stitch by hand, but it is possible to use the machine. Betsy did, with beautiful results.

When your tablecloth is the size you want, cut a backing material roughly to match. Trim down to within the ¼-inch seam allowance. With right sides facing, sew around the entire edge, but leave about a foot open for reversing. Carefully clip all the seam allowance at all the points along the outside edge so they will take shape later. Turn the cloth right side out and press.

Topstitch at least the outermost hexagon edges of the table-cloth to get sharp corners. Stitch by hand or machine. But consider hand-stitching more. Betsy quilted by hand around each ring to keep the patchwork top and backing from separating and to create a beautiful quilt contour.

turtle ornament

TURTLE ORNAMENTS

Make a template the size of the finished turtle. On the wrong side of fabric trace the template once, flop it over, and trace it again in the opposite direction. Cut out ¼ inch from the line. On the face of one turtle shape, pin ribbon or any other trim in position, and stitch. Pin the front and back together, face to face, with a loop of rickrack placed in the seam, as shown, for a hanger. Stitch and stuff like a pillow.

Any animal ornament can be made like this. Use animal shapes that you find in this book, like the rabbit, or invent your own.

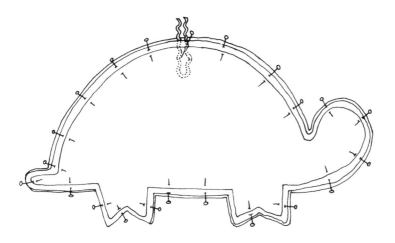

STRIP-PATCHED TURTLE

Make a template the size of the finished turtle and use it to prepare two fabric turtle shapes as described for the Turtle Ornaments. One shape will become a decorated turtle front and the other a plain back.

Using the parallel-strip-patch method outlined on page 43, prepare a turtle shell just slightly larger than the area to be covered on the turtle front.

Lay the prepared strip-patched shell in position on the front of the turtle, turn under the bottom edge of the shell, and top-stitch ribbon over it.

Assemble the Strip-Patched Turtle with the same procedure described for the Turtle Ornaments. When the turtle is stuffed, give him a button eye and a bow around his neck.

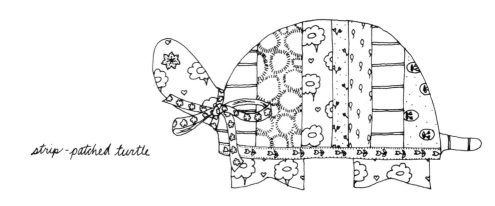

strip-patched turtle

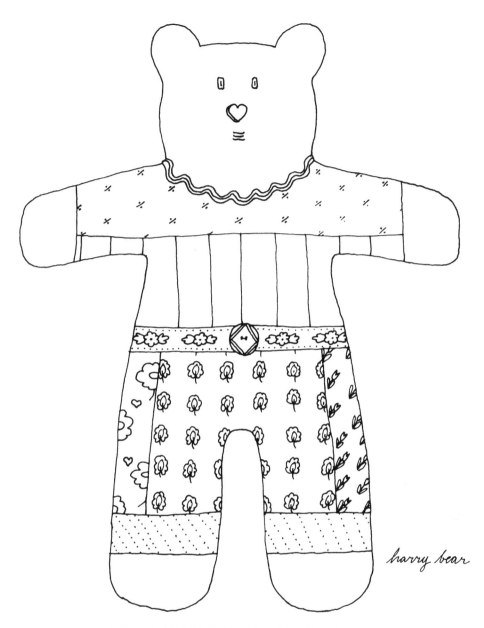

harry bear

THE PATCHWORK BEARS

The patchwork bears are both cut from the same outline, but, because the female bear is made of a fuzzy material, she appears to have a different shape. Harry Bear's clothing was patched together and appliquéd onto the front section of his brown cotton body before he was constructed. Pola Bear was sewn and stuffed before she was dressed. Both bears are built entirely with machine stitching with the extra trims on the faces added by hand.

Harry Bear

To create Harry Bear, mark his two main pattern pieces by tracing the bear silhouette twice on the wrong side of pieces of brown fabric. Cut out, making sure to leave the ¼-inch seam allowance. Next, construct two 5″ × 7″ patchwork panels for Harry's clothes according to the instructions in the strip-patching section on page 43. You will also need rickrack for his neckline, ribbon for his belt, and extra strips of fabric for the cuffs of his pants.

The Front Panel   With a pencil or chalk, draw the outlines for Harry's clothes on the right side of one of the main pattern pieces. Pin the patched pieces for the shirt and pants in place on Harry's front. Turn this unit of two pinned layers face down, and trim the patchwork pieces to match the silhouette of the foundation piece. Make sure to leave ¼-inch seam allowance. Turn the bear so the right side is facing front again. The patchwork material should just cover the lines indicating the sleeve and pants length. Pin an additional strip of fabric, with each edge folded under, in place over the bottom of the pants legs for the cuffs. Trim the neckline ¼ inch above the line you have drawn for it and cut notches in the neckline semicircle so that it will hem easily. Fold under and pin. The neckline, as with the sleeves and cuffs, should just cover the guideline. Pin or glue rickrack around the curve of the neckline. Pin a ribbon across the waistline where the shirt and pants meet.

Topstitch all pinned areas: the rickrack neckline, the sleeve lengths, and both edges of the ribbon belt and cuffs. Remove the pins and press Harry on the wrong side.

Final Construction   To construct Harry Bear's body, place his decorated front half face to face with the plain fabric for his back half, pin, and stitch. Begin stitching on the bear's side somewhere near his belt. Leave a three-inch opening in the bear's side for reversing and stuffing his form. Before you reverse him, however, cut tiny notches around his outline to help

HARRY BEAR: *all edges of clothing are hemmed and topstitched*

the curved edges take form. Be careful not to cut through the stitching. Reverse the bear by gently pulling the inside out through the hole you have left in his side. You may use a crochet hook or the blunt end of a pencil to help free his ears or any other area that is hard to get at.

Stuff Harry with Dacron Fiberfil, old stockings, or rags until he is firm. Sew up the stuffing hole with tiny hand stitches.

Mark Harry's facial features with a pencil or chalk. Using regular sewing thread doubled, make small horizontal straight stitches to fill in the eyes and mouth. Use vertical stitches for the pupils of his eyes, a button for his nose, and a button for his belt buckle.

pola bear

Pola Bear

Cut, stitch, and stuff Pola Bear's body, as described for Harry Bear, before you clothe her. Her dress will be removable.

This time, use fake fur for the bear's body, beads for her eyes, and a button for her nose.

To make the dress bodice, line off the neckline and the armholes directly on the bear's shape. Trace this area onto paper to make a template. Cut two identical pieces from fabric leaving the standard ¼-inch seam allowance. Clip and turn under the neck and armholes and sew in place with small blindstitches.

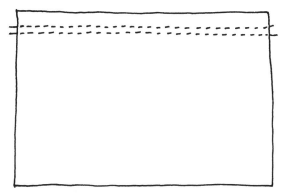

POLA BEAR'S SKIRT : *double row of machine basting*

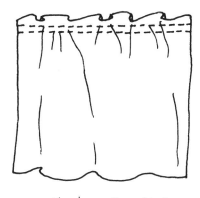

gathering the skirt

adding the waistband

Construct the skirt of her dress by making two strip-patched panels for the front and back. See the strip-patching directions on page 43. Run a double line of machine basting along the width of the patched panels. Pull on the basting threads to gather the fabric and to reduce the width to fit the bodice. Pin ribbon over the gathered stitch line on both pieces. Topstitch only along the bottom edge of the ribbon. Trim away any fabric that shows above the top edge of the ribbon.

Pin the top of each waistband over the bottom of each bodice piece. All fabric should be right side up. Topstitch along the top edge of the ribbon to join the bodice and skirt.

Place the two completed sides of the dress face to face and pin at the shoulders and side seams. Try the dress on the bear's form and make any necessary adjustments. When you are satisfied with the fit, remove and do final stitching. Reverse the dress and hold it up to Pola or try it on her again to determine the hem length. Pin and topstitch the hem with a straight or zigzag stitch. Add a spray of fabric flowers to her waist.

joining the front and back   *the completed dress front*

DOLL WITH PARALLEL-STRIP-PATCHED DRESS AND HANDBAG

Make this cheerful doll as shown on page 114 to any size you want and clothe her in a whimsical strip-patched outfit.

Draw a template to the exact size of the finished doll and use it to prepare two fabric base pieces for the front and back of the doll. Follow the directions for the Turtle Ornaments on page 105. The finished doll, just like the ornaments, will have a decorated front panel and a plain back.

Outline the doll's dress on the right side of the front panel; using the parallel-strip-patch method described on page 43, build a piece of fabric for the doll's dress. Trim the dress shape to within the ¼-inch seam allowance, and then decorate the strips with rickrack. Use small dabs of fabric glue to hold the rickrack in place while you stitch it in position.

Affix the decorated dress to the doll's front panel and do the final assembly, using the method described for Harry Bear on page 108.

When the doll is assembled and stuffed, make hair by cutting lengths of three-strand crewel or needlepoint yarn. Draw a center part down the middle of the doll's head. Attach each length with an embroidery needle by taking a small stitch under the guideline and pulling the yarn through so half remains on each side. Tie into pigtails with baby-size rickrack, trim evenly, and tack hair to the head with a few small stitches of thread. If you wish, cut several of the long strands shorter in front for bangs.

For a necklace, thread small glass beads onto a doubled length of thread (quilting thread would be best) and tie. Slip beads into position around the doll's neck and stitch in several places to hold. Sew on a face with medium-sized beads for eyes and tiny buttons for the nose and mouth, or embroider a face. Make a handbag out of scraps of strip patching. Fold a piece of material in half, face to face, and stitch down two sides. Reverse and press. Attach a rickrack handle and sew on a bead to look like a clasp. Stitch the bag to the doll's hand.

doll with parallel-strip-patched dress and handbag

THE GINGHAM CAT

Who ever heard of a gingham cat? Sitting together one after-
noon, Betsy and I charted out our ideal beast.

Betsy collected a variety of checked fabrics for the body,
felt and buttons for the face, nylon cording for the whiskers,
and white piqué for the paws. She built the main body and tail
separately by machine and added the facial features, claws, and
stuffed tail by hand. The fabric nose and tongue are glued in
place.

Betsy was not satisfied with her construction of the cat's tail.
The directions for how she did it are included, although she
hopes that someone will devise a better solution. Perhaps it
will be you.

The front and back panels are each composed of nineteen
1½ -inch squares and two triangular ears 1½ " × 1½ " × 1".
The front and back panels are joined by a chain of twenty-four
1½ -inch squares with one 1" × 1½ " shape for the space be-

the gingham cat

tween the ears. The 1-inch edge of this one shape runs with the length of the chain; remember this when adding it to the others. Also, it is crucial to build the front and back panels facing in opposite directions so they can be joined properly later.

The tail is made of four rows of shapes of diminishing widths. The length of each shape is always 1½ inches. The shapes' widths measure like this: row one (closest to the body and the row that will be joined to the body later), top edge 1½ inches, bottom edge 1¼ inches; row two, top edge 1¼ inches, bottom edge 1 inch; row three, top edge 1 inch, bottom edge ¾ inch; row four, top edge ¾ inch, bottom edge ½ inch. Cut four pieces of each shape. The tip of the cat's tail is a ½-inch square.

To construct the gingham cat, complete the patchwork front and back panels and the chain of squares. Add the face to the front panel. Pink felt cheeks with tiny red French knots may be hand-stitched in place and stuffed with a tiny bit of cotton or Fiberfil. Thread short lengths of the nylon cord into a tapestry needle, knot the end, and pull the cord through the cheeks so the knot is hidden. This will form whiskers. Next, join the front panel of the cat to the long chain of squares by pinning right sides together. Begin by joining the odd 1″ × 1½″ shape in between the ears. Continue by pinning along the 1½-inch sides of the triangular ears and around the rest of the cat until the chain of squares is closed. Machine stitch in place and also join the two ends of chain together. Next, join the back panel to the free side of the strip of squares, right sides facing. Pin and stitch, but leave two or three squares open along the bottom of the stomach for reversing and stuffing. Turn the cat right side out, stuff, and blindstitch closed.

To make the tail, cut the pieces as described and join along the 1½-inch seams. Center and join the diminishing-length strips as shown. With right sides facing, fold and stitch the two outer edges to form a four-sided tube. Add the ½-inch square to seal the end of the tail. Reverse and stuff into tubular shape. Trim the two opposite topmost squares so the tail will hang off the body as pictured. Turn the tail hem inward, pin in place on the back of the cat, and blindstitch in place.

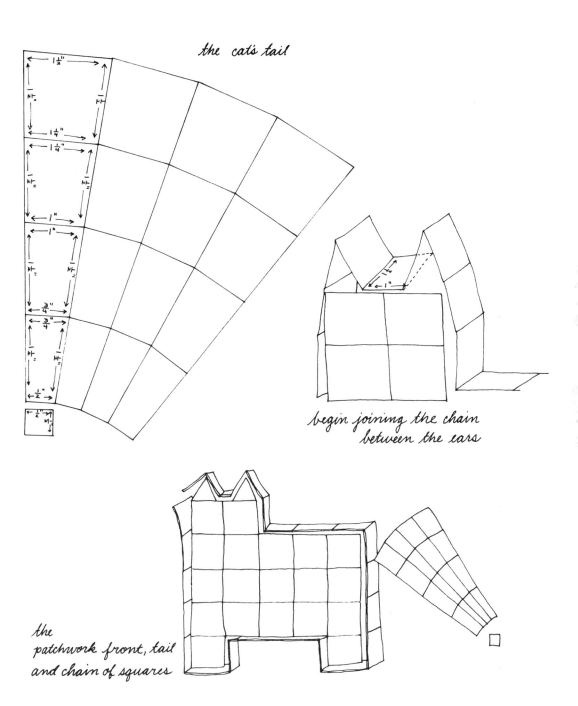

the cat's tail

$1\frac{1}{2}"$

$1\frac{1}{4}"$

$1\frac{1}{4}"$

$1"$

$1"$

$\frac{3}{4}"$

$\frac{3}{4}"$

$\frac{1}{2}"$

$\frac{1}{2}"$

begin joining the chain
between the ears

the
patchwork front, tail
and chain of squares

THE EASY APPLIQUÉ SATCHEL

This playful, all-purpose bag can be created in a jiffy if you use a sewing machine. Made of cotton duck and lined with felt, it is sewn with a zigzag stitch for strength and speed.

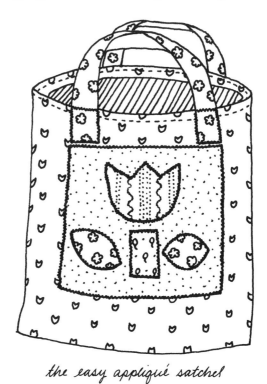

the easy appliqué satchel

First prepare two 8″ × 9″ inside panels of light cotton as the background for the appliqué tulips. These will go on the back and the front of the bag. Cut the tulip pieces on the sewing line, pin them in place on the background, and stitch.

Cut out two canvas panels whose finished size will be 11½″ × 13″. Leave an inch more than the standard ¼-inch allowance along the top edge of each panel to conceal the lining later.

Center, pin, and sew one tulip-appliquéd panel to each of the larger canvas panels.

fold top hem of finished appliqué panel over the lining and topstitch

zigzag handle in position

do final construction by sewing completed panels together face to face

Cut two pieces of felt to match the canvas panels, omitting the extra inch on top.

Lay one canvas panel, complete with appliqué, right side up over each felt sheet. Fold the extra inch of duck over the top of the felt. Pin in place. Topstitch the hem. Do the same with the back of bag.

The bag has two handles each measuring $1\frac{1}{4}'' \times 15''$. For each, fold a $2\frac{1}{2}'' \times 15''$ piece of duck in half with the right sides facing. Stitch two sides, leaving one of the short sides open. Reverse, press, and finish off as you would complete a belt (see Patchwork Belt on page 133). Pin each handle in position on the surface of a duck panel and zigzag in place so that the stitching forms a rectangle, as shown.

Assemble the bag by sewing the two duck panels, complete with felt lining and handles, face to face, on three sides. Leave the top edge open. Clip the corners and reverse.

SUMMER PARALLEL-STRIP-PATCH BAG

I used this bag all summer, gave it a rinse in mild bleach and soap suds, hung it up to dry, and it was ready for another season.

Make two strip-patched areas according to the directions on page 43 . The body of the finished strip-patched bag should measure 10½ " × 16" and the flap should be 10½ " × 7¾ ". Be sure to leave the usual ¼ -inch seam allowance all around during construction.

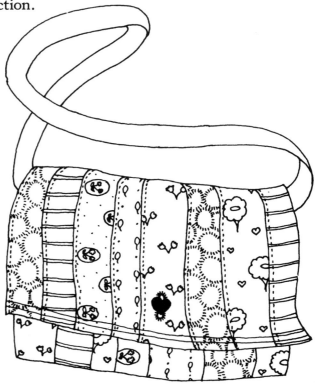

the summer parallel-strip-patch bag

Cut two pieces of lining fabric to match the strip-patched panels. Consider denim or corduroy if you want a washable bag, felt if you don't mind dry cleaning. Join the lining to the stripped areas by sewing face to face as if you were making a pillow. Turn right side out, press, stitch openings closed, and topstitch around all sides on both completed panels.

Make small quilting stitches down each strip for strength and decoration as shown in the drawing of the finished bag.

Place the 10½-inch edge of the body face to face with the 10½-inch edge of the flap and stitch together. You should be sewing with the lining out.

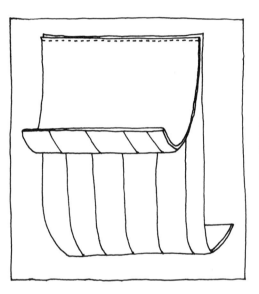

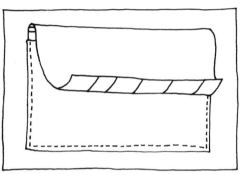

inside out with sides stitched

joining the body and the flap

Open the bag out flat and fold the body panel in half—with the lining out—to form the bag. Pin along the side seams. Make sure you have folded so that the front of the body is slightly shorter than the back of the body. This is so the flap will fall properly when the bag is completed.

Straight stitch down both of the pinned sides. Remove the pins, trim the corners on the diagonal, and reverse the bag.

To make handles, use fabric from the legs of old jeans or any other strong material. If you do use jeans, you may have to make the handle in two pieces. Cut or build a piece 2″ × 39″. Fold in half, face to face, and stitch around two open sides (the long side and one short side) ⅛ inch from the edges. Trim the corners and turn right side out by pulling handle through open end. When the strap is reversed, press with a hot iron. Push in the seam allowance at the open end and stitch it closed. Pin each end of the strap over the outside side seams of the bag so there are 4½ inches left between the bottom of strap and the bottom of the bag on each side (see the diagram). Join the straps to the body by topstitching 1/16 inch in from the edge of the strap to form a closed rectangle.

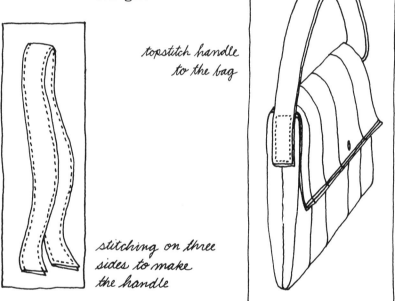

topstitch handle
to the bag

stitching on three
sides to make
the handle

Fold the flap into the correct position (if it isn't already there) to determine the correct button and buttonhole placement. The buttonhole is made on the flap. It should be centered at least 1 inch from the bottom edge of the flap. Make a small vertical cut with a sharp scissors through the flap and its lining. Make sure the button you have chosen will be able to fit through. Buttonhole stitch (see page 50) through the two layers of the flap to bind the edges of the incision. When the buttonhole is complete, fold the bag into correct position again. Using a pencil or chalk, mark a dot onto the body of the bag through the buttonhole. Sew the button on this dot.

THE APPLIQUÉ STRAWBERRY POUCH

Let a flower- or fruit-embroidered ribbon inspire you to make a playful drawstring pouch. Stitch the appliqué strawberry by hand, and construct the bag by machine.

the appliqué strawberry pouch

Cut an oval shape out of shirt cardboard approximately 3″ × 5″ for the bottom of the bag.

Cut a corresponding oval with a ¾-inch seam allowance from a printed fabric.

To make the cylindrical shape, measure the circumference of the cardboard oval with a tape measure, and, adding a seam allowance, cut a piece for the body of the bag from the same printed fabric. The height of the panel should be 7½ inches and the width should wrap comfortably and completely around the cardboard base.

Cut two pieces of felt for a lining to match the printed oval and body panel. The depth of the felt body lining should be increased by ¾ inch so it can be folded into a decorative lip later.

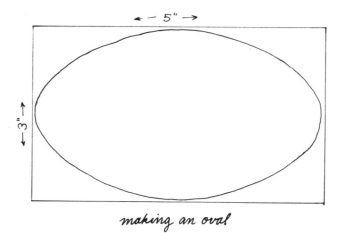

making an oval

Appliqué your fruit or flower motif to the front side of body panel. Appliqué by hand. Consider using glass beads as decorative trim, but be sure to make a knot in the thread on the back after each bead is applied for safety and strength. There is no need to cut the thread each time; just continue stitching.

Sew the edges of green satin ribbon together to form tubular leaves for the strawberry.

Also use similar tubes as loops beginning one inch from the top edge of the bag to guide the drawstring ribbon. Be sure they are roomy enough for ribbon to pass through. Sew the loops, eight in all, at one-inch intervals around the outside of the bag.

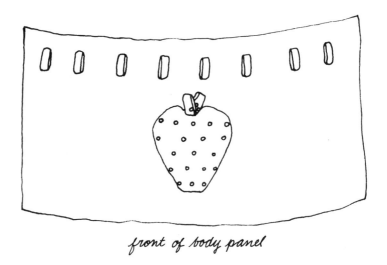

front of body panel

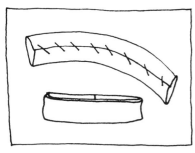

making tubular leaves out of satin ribbon

finished appliqué panel with lining

When you have completed the strawberry appliqué panel, place it, right side up, over the felt so that ⅜ inch of felt sticks over the top edge. Fold the felt over the front of the appliqué panel (which will be the outside of the bag) and hem with tiny blind stitches to form a finished edge.

Fold the strawberry panel in half—lining side out—and stitch down the side to form a tube.

To make the base, sandwich the cardboard oval between the oval felt and the oval printed material, print side out. Stitch around the perimeter of the cardboard as close to it as you can. With printed fabric sides together, pin the covered oval to the base tube. Ease the material as you work so it is well distributed. Stitch (again) close to the cardboard. Clip the seam allowance in the curves and reverse the bag.

Thread the drawstring ribbon, decorative side out, through the loops so it circles the bag one-and-a-half-times. Draw each end of the ribbon out and stitch together to complete the handle.

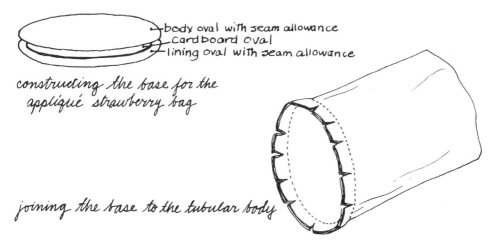

body oval with seam allowance
cardboard oval
lining oval with seam allowance

constructing the base for the appliqué strawberry bag

joining the base to the tubular body

THE CRAZY QUILT BAG

For an eye-catching, special-occasion accessory, consider stitching the Crazy Quilt Bag. The diameter of the bag before it was gathered on the ring was a sizable twenty-six inches. The finished bag is considerably smaller once all the sides draw in, but the large base size allows the bag to be conveniently roomy inside. Choose your own bag size.

Cut a fabric base from an old sheet, piece of muslin, or any other expendable lightweight material and follow the instructions in the crazy quilt section on page 60 to construct the crazy quilt top.

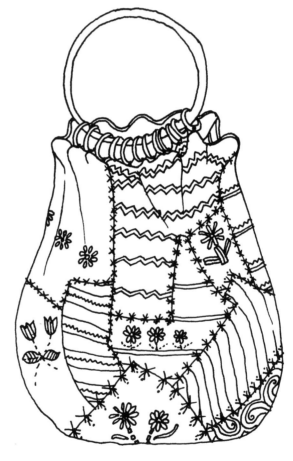

the crazy quilt bag

When it is complete with decorative stitching, add a lining as if you were adding a pillow back. In other words, cut lining material to the size of the completed crazy quilt top. Sew the two fabrics together face to face. Do not completely stitch around the circle, but leave an open space for reversing the bag. When the right sides are facing out, turn in the open section, stitch closed, and press the unit with a warm iron. Then, with machine straight stitches, topstitch around the entire circumference of the bag about ¼ inch in from the outside edge. This will add strength and give the crazy quilting a beautifully finished look.

crazy quilt bag
with ribbon
drawstring handle

If you have been lucky enough to discover an appropriate circular handle in a thrift shop or trimming store, now is the time to attach it. But if you are without a handle, you can devise something wonderful out of ribbons. Choose medium-width, decorative ribbon (or ribbons) that blend well with the materials you have used for your crazy quilting. Select embroidered satin or striped grosgrain if your bag is made of mostly ornate or formal neckties. Whatever you use, make sure the tones of the materials are consistent with each other. Avoid brightly colored, primitively decorated ribbon if your bag is dark and Victorian. On the other hand, if you have chosen delicately colored prints for your bag, black ribbon with gold threads would certainly be too heavy.

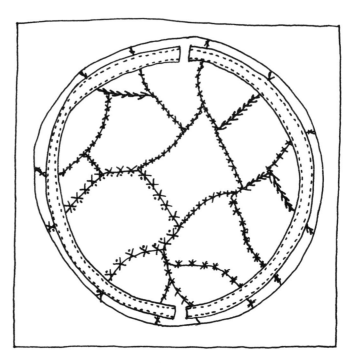

the crazy quilt bag with ribbon casings

Once you have made the choice, make sure to purchase or collect enough ribbon in a suitable width to go around the outside edge on the bag for a drawstring casing. Pin the ribbon in two sections, as shown, around the perimeter on the crazy quilt side. Fold under the cut ends of the ribbon for neatness and to prevent fraying, leaving a small space between each ribbon length. Topstitch each ribbon along the long sides only. Do not stitch down the ends or you will close off the casings. Stitch close to the edge of the ribbons, however, to leave the tunnels as wide as possible. You will also need a separate ribbon to thread through the casing. It should be long enough to form a comfortable handle. Thread this ribbon through the tunnels so it circles the bag twice. Tie or stitch the ends of the ribbon together and draw the bag closed by pulling ribbon through each space between the casings. You can also use the handle casing suggested for the Strawberry Pouch on page 124 or invent your own.

THE LOG CABIN NAME BAG

I made this Log Cabin Name Bag for Betsy, but now I think I'll make one for myself. The wooden handles come from a craft supply store, but they can also be ordered as knitting bag handles through mail order catalogues or cut from a worn-out bag un-earthed in a thrift shop or at a garage sale.

This patchwork, appliqué, and quilt bag is made of front and back panels measuring 12 inches high by 16½ inches long. Each panel, with an extra two-inch seam allowance on the top, is constructed in a standard quilt sandwich. For details, turn to page 55. The front of the bag is appliquéd with a patchwork cabin, the middle layer is Dacron batting, and the backing—or lining of the bag—is a fabric that coordinates with the appliqué design. The bag is decorated by hand for beauty but constructed by machine for strength.

the log cabin name bag

Follow the directions for assembling a quilt on page 55 and baste together the layers to construct the front and back panels of the bag. This assemblage will not include the appliqué decorations. These will be added later.

Next, construct the name plate, or central panel, for the log cabin. Carefully draw the outline of the name plate and the name you are using to size on a sheet of tracing paper. The length of the name and the size of the letters that you choose will determine the size of the name plate. If the name is especially long, consider using initials. Pin the tracing paper outline in place on the front of a piece of fabric with dressmaker's carbon in between. Using a tracing wheel or, if the letters are too small, the pointed end of a crochet hook, press hard and trace the letters and the name plate outline, transferring them to the fabric. Make sure you have chosen a color of tracing carbon that contrasts with the fabric so you will have a clear image. You will stitch the name in later when the finished log cabin has been affixed to the bag top.

Next, place dressmaker's carbon against the back of the fabric (by slipping it underneath) and trace over boundaries of the name plate with the crochet hook so you will have it marked on the back of the fabric as well as the front.

Continue by constructing the log cabin. Make two ¾-inch-wide strips the height of the name plate (see the diagram) and sew on as you would any other patchwork element. Next, cut two ¾-inch-wide strips the length of the name plate including the new additions on each side. Sew these in place.

Cut two more ¾-inch strips to the new height of the name plate and patch in place. Cut and sew two more according to the newest measurements for the final top and bottom. You have

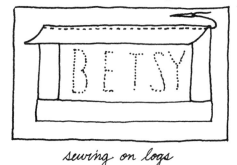

sewing on logs

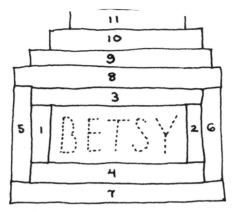

the sequence of adding logs

now constructed a log cabin. You will need three more strips, also ¾ inch wide, of diminishing lengths for the roof. Look at the Betsy bag to understand the general proportions and then cut yours in relation to the size of your log cabin. Sew the strips in place. Baste all outside hems under and set the cabin aside for a few minutes.

Cut a ground plane for the log cabin and the trees. Pin or baste this area in place on the panel you have chosen for the handbag front.

where to quilt

Pin or baste the completed name plate log cabin in place over the ground plane. Using tiny running stitches, appliqué around the edge of the house including the roof and the ground plane. You are appliquéing and quilting the house in one motion without the use of quilting frame or hoop. This is possible because the bag is so much smaller and more manageable than a quilt. It is a good idea to use quilting thread, if it is available, for this stitching because it is strong and resists tangles. Place little running stitches around the inside of each rectangular strip on the cabin.

Next, appliqué the trees. Cut tree trunks and the treetops and hem the edges. Press. Pin the trunks down first and then the treetops so they overlap the trunks slightly. Sew with tiny running stitches. When you have about two inches left open on a treetop, consider pushing a small amount of stuffing through the opening to give the treetop a little fullness. Use a pencil or crochet hook to distribute the filling. Continue stitching until the treetop is sealed.

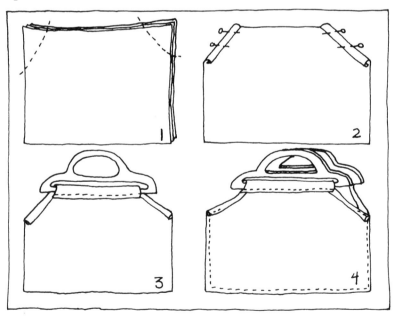

adding the handles

Add the handles to each panel by cutting the top of the bag into diagonals as shown and then clipping out some of the batting to reduce the bulk. Turn under the diagonal edges and pin or baste. Thread the tops of the bag through the slits of the wooden handles, fold under, and hem.

To construct the bag, place the front and back panels—complete with wooden handles—face to face, and pin. Begin stitching on one side about 5 inches from the top of the bag and end off stitching in the same place on the opposite side. Reverse the bag.

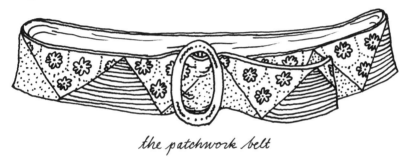

the patchwork belt

THE PATCHWORK BELT

Denim clothes look great with warm colors and patchwork, so what could be more natural than this triangle belt? The modules here are cut from the same template used for the triangular shapes of the Basic Patchwork Quilted Pillow on page 68. Use three different printed materials, two alternating along the length of one edge and one running continuously the length of the other. Following the directions on page 73, patch together triangles. The patchwork belt top is backed with denim salvaged from an old pair of pants, to give the belt strength. Complete the pieced top first and then sew it face to face with the denim, leaving one end open. Turn the belt right side out, tuck in the open end, and stitch it closed. Use the outside edge of your patchwork as the stitch guideline. Quilt the layers together following along the contours of the triangles. Make an extra long belt and tie it closed, or make it closer to your waist size and use a pretty plastic buckle.

THE PATCH POCKET APRON

Make a million-dollar apron with dime-store handkerchiefs. Melanie Zwerling used a basic commercial pattern to build a denim base and patched delicately flowered pockets on it. The neck and waist are tied with coordinated ribbon and all top stitching shown in the drawing by dotted lines is done in pink. If you want to make a man's apron, consider substituting bandana scarves for the pockets with appropriately colored neck and waist fasteners and top stitching. For a more formal apron, try making crazy quilt necktie patch pockets (see page 60) and use the skinny necktie ends to secure the waist and neck.

the patch pocket apron

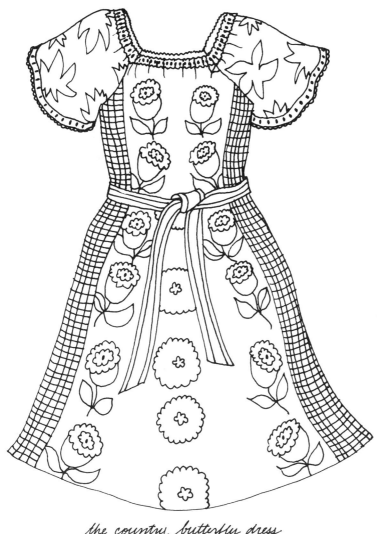

the country butterfly dress

THE COUNTRY BUTTERFLY DRESS

I made a nostalgic country dress with butterfly sleeves for my-self by patching together old linen toweling, gingham, and flowered cotton to fit a standard peasant dress pattern, intended for use with one overall fabric. The fabric I wanted to use for the main pattern piece didn't quite fit the pattern company's plan, so I had to improvise. As with the café curtains on page 81, I patched together small amounts of material to invent the right size fabric. The body of the dress is a flowered central panel bordered by gingham. The butterfly sleeves are cut from a complementary third print. Instead of using traditional bias tape on the inside of the neckline to build the elastic casing, I substituted decorative ribbon, which I stitched on the outside instead. The sleeves are edged with a scalloped trim, which could also hold elastic, but I decided to leave them loose and flowing. The waist is tied with a striped grosgrain ribbon.

If I hadn't been so in love with the central flowered toweling, I probably never would have invented the butterfly dress. I have since made myself another using the same principle. The second time, however, I fitted together offbeat materials—not from necessity but because I enjoyed the results. So don't be afraid to let your materials guide you. Take a cue from a length of fabric or a flowered ribbon and devise something terrific!

PATCHWORK KIMONO

The classic kimono is a welcome friend from the East. Wonderful to throw on when you wake up, terrific to wrap in after a shower, and super to wear for just relaxing, it's an easy garment to sew. It flatters all sorts of shapes without the use of darts, tucks, or fancy tailoring. Make one as a gift for yourself or someone else.

Here is a garment so simple to construct that you can spend your time choosing and patching fabrics instead of installing buttonholes and zippers. The kimono is made of two whimsically different prints. The main body and pocket pieces are a multicolored patchwork-printed fabric. The sleeves, belt, trim, and pocket flap are a totally unexpected two-tone fabric. The sleeve and bottom hems were pinned in place and topstitched with a double row of wide machine zigzagging.

When my father-in-law brought this kimono on a visit to California, our mutual relative, Betsy, wisely added a grosgrain ribbon in the neck for easy hanging and embroidery floss loops in the side seams to keep the belt attached.

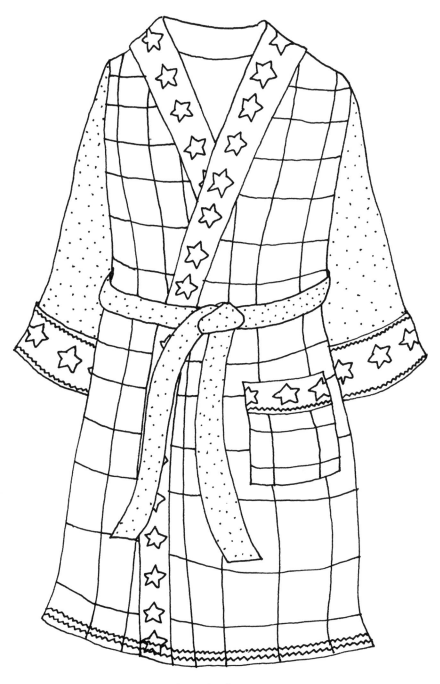

patchwork kimono

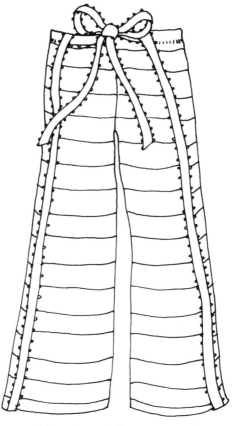

delicate patchwork pants

MELANIE'S DELICATE PATCHWORK PANTS

The elegant pants by Melanie Zwerling are made of horizontal strips of white sheeting and unbleached muslin. This particular pair is sewn from a one-size-fits-all commercial pattern. Each finished strip, 2¼ inches wide, was marked with ruler and pencil directly on the fabric and cut with pinking shears. Patched together (see patchwork section on page 42) to form the overall yardage requirements, they were then laid out and cut according to the pattern. The outside edging and waist tie bands are made of luxurious black-and-rust satin ribbon. This wonderful muslin and sheeting combination can be used effectively with any pattern for loose-fitting, easily constructed pants.

FRIENDLY ANIMAL APPLIQUÉD CLOTHES FOR CHILDREN

Give a child a pet when you appliqué a friendly beast on the bib of overalls or a pinafore. You can enliven a standard commercial pattern with thoughtfully chosen fabrics, ribbons, trims, and a whimsical animal shape. Use the rabbit on page 140, the dog below, or any other animal in this book, or invent your own.

Patch the bib together first and then add the appliqué animal with tiny buttonhole stitching and magical trims. Complete the garment according to the pattern instructions. Add ribbon to the straps and waistband before you do the final sewing. Consider piecing a playful patchwork skirt, also shown on page 140, of your own design based on a favorite pinafore pattern.

Both the pinafore and overalls were masterfully sewn by Vicki Rosenberg.

dog appliqué overalls

rabbit appliqué pinafore

THE PATCHWORK SUPERSHIRT

Kendra Adams turned an everyday tunic top into a Supershirt with some patch magic. You can devise an equally spectacular creation with your own hands if you spend time arranging materials and stitch only when you have found a combination that gives you visual pleasure. As with all magic, it's what you see that counts. Choose soft prints, floral ribbon, and old lace for a delicate country look. Use muted geometrics and simple trims for comfortable, easy elegance. If you want to create a formal feeling, select velvet, silk, and ornate decorations.

Cut the shirt base from a loose fitting, pullover pattern. Use the same basic fabric for the body, sleeves, and facings. Apply the decorative fabrics and trims to the front section of the shirt before you do final construction. Kendra recommends working from the center outward. Look at the diagrams. Each new fabric, with the standard ¼-inch seam allowance, is slipped under the preceding one. The materials are pinned securely in place with all top edges turned under neatly and then topstitched. The sleeves are trimmed in the same way, repeating fabrics from the front of the shirt.

the patchwork
supershirt

pinning

topstitching

CRAZY QUILT SKIRT

The secret to this project is to cover a skirt you already own, although there is no reason why you can't work over a muslin or other lightweight skirt made from a commercial pattern. The advantages of working over something from your closet, should you be lucky enough to have something simply cut and ready for transformation, are clear. Besides recycling an old garment, you save a bit of time and energy to work on the actual crazy quilting. If you have chosen a base skirt that fits well, you will be sure ahead of time that the measurements are correct. An A-line or flared skirt of lightweight material (you will be adding another few layers, don't forget, so the finished piece will be much heavier) is best suited to this. It should lie flat, without gathers, because if it is full you will have trouble keeping the patches from buckling and much of the embroidery work will be hidden by folds. On this particular skirt, Betsy used old silk ties—not just outsides, but pretty linings and labels as well as scraps of velvet and lace. She pinned the pieces in place, making sure they overlapped by at least ¼ inch, and basted them down with a stitch that was long on the underside and short on the surface. In this case, the basting was not removed and the embroidery covered the surface tacking stitches. She carefully featherstitched (for embroidery stitches turn to page 49) with doubled sewing thread in pastel colors around the surface edge of each patch and then covered the waistband with an antique embroidered ribbon. I added crewel flowers freehand to random patches (thinking mostly about where they'd be shown off best) and added three rows of velvet ribbon and yarn cross-stitching around the hem. All in all, it's a knockout skirt and I feel that it generates a lot of excitement and curiosity around me whenever I wear it. This particular skirt has a formal but livable feeling because of the richness of the materials, which are silk (printed, striped, and solid) and velvet (patches and ribbons), and because of the use of the embroidery techniques (featherstitching around patches, yarn flowers in patches, and cross-stitching) around the hem. Certainly a piece of clothing that takes so

the crazy quilt skirt

much time and thought to make (this one, as I said, was a two-person endeavor) deserves to be used for special occasions—but don't make the mistake many of our grandmothers did and just put it away in a trunk thinking it too good to use—ever.

THE ART OF PATCHING, OR INVENT YOUR OWN DENIM DECO

There are several reasons to patch clothing—to hide a flaw, to strengthen a worn area, to prevent a potential hole, or just to brighten something bland. The best patching I know fulfills a little of each need. How complete is a repair patch unless made of a pretty fabric or cut in pleasant shape? What good are decorative additions without reinforcing or protective elements? People have been patching their garments instinctively since the invention of clothing, but it was only when I made my first attempts to repair my own clothes and saw the disappointingly uninspired results that I realized that good patching is an unrecognized art. The only way I was going to learn to produce sturdy, yet visually exciting patches was to watch how other people tackled the problem and to experiment.

My friend Brenda, who had begun doing lovely patchwork on a favorite pair of well-worn jeans, seemed to be on the right track. Together, we explored the question "What is good patching?" We concentrated our patch investigation on denim clothing.

Cotton denim, worn by so many people, for so many purposes, for so many years, improves with wear. Double-stitched for strength, a denim garment is stiff with sizing when new. But as the item is worn and washed, the fabric softens and the cotton shapes itself to its wearer. Invariably, just as a pair of jeans or a jacket is beginning to feel like a faithful friend, it springs a leak. Because personal repair needs vary, we wanted to design patches that would be useful to everyone. Now that cotton fibers are becoming so scarce and expensive, we felt it was even more urgent to extend the life of our clothing. But aside from devising utilitarian repairs, we wanted to create patches that would add life and personality to our jeans. We had discovered that we preferred wearing jeans that were artfully repaired rather than disposing of them and having to start again with a new, ordinary pair.

Fabric is not regenerative, so once a garment like jeans starts wearing thin, patching may become an ongoing process until

jeans for Nick

you have slowly covered all of the weakened material, and almost all of your jeans. Brenda worked an entire summer at patching the seat of a pair of dungarees. The fabric was in a very worn condition when she began to repair them, so as she was patching one hole, it was just a matter of time before another spot would break through. It took several weeks before the patch reinforcing joined with the damaged areas in enough places to become a new and stronger fabric. Each patch, however, was so thoughtfully considered and carefully crafted that the finished section was unexpectedly dynamic and fluid. Brenda prepared patches the same way she would make appliqués (see page 44), by cutting, hemming, pressing, and sewing a shape in position on the surface of the worn garment, but she used the fabric doubled for strength. She managed to avoid uncomfortable padded buildup by abutting each addition rather than overlapping. The jeans, now enjoying a glorious second life, may need further repairs in the future, but each new patch will only make the revitalizing process the more exciting. These pants are no longer just "repaired" by patching. They are covered with such beautiful appliqué shapes, subtle fabrics, and delicate stitching that they are a whole new creation.

Types of Patching

There are two approaches to consider when beginning to patch —patch by hand and patch by machine. Both have their own separate advantages and purposes.

Machine Patching

Machine patching is excellent for garments that will open up and lie flat like shirts and jean jackets. It's also recommended for areas that can be fed through the sewing machine in a continuous motion, like ragged cuffs or splitting seams. Machine patching is fast, but more important, it's strong. It's great for reviving raveling edges, adding patchwork cuffs, or decorating with ribbon. The density of the machine stitching, however, produces a toughness that is not recommended for knee patches or worn-through seats; it makes the knees stiff and the seat uncomfortably thick. But this stitch density can also be made to work for you in other areas. When you add fabric edging to lengthen sleeves or pants legs, the machine stitching will encourage the new addition to fall properly. If you are lengthening clothes for a child, add only the top of the cuff by machine. Hem the bottom edge by hand for easy adjustment.

Hand Patching

If you choose to patch by hand you will have a portable project. In addition, you will be using a technique that allows you to repair areas that cannot be easily reached by machine. You will be able to ease the new fabric onto the damaged surface as you stitch so that the new patch is sculpted to the shape of the garment. Hand patching is a personal touch that gives your clothes distinction and expression. Happily, everyone's stitching and choice of materials is wonderfully different.

Any soft, washable medium-weave fabric will work as patch material, but I have found that carefully chosen cotton (and

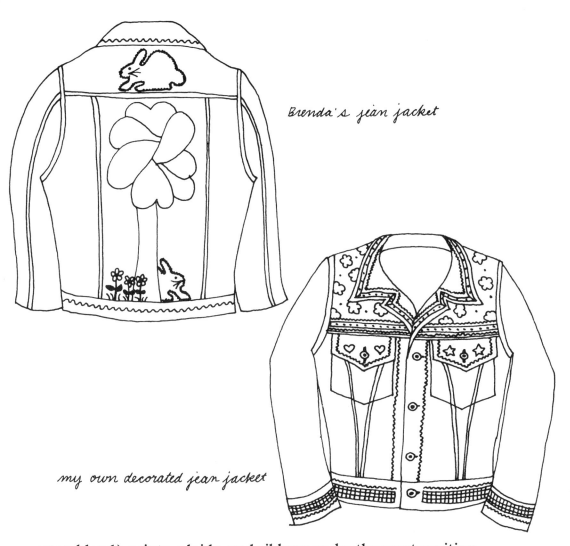

Brenda's jean jacket

my own decorated jean jacket

cotton blend) prints, plaids, and ribbons make the most exciting patches. Bright, bold patterns seem to pop visually from the surface of worn, paled-out denim. You may like that effect, but if you want to maintain a subtle, unified surface, choose only gently patterned, nonelectric fabrics. Brenda decorated Nick's jeans with predominantly plaid and geometric shapes and look how beautifully the patches sit on the denim. After bleaching my own jean jacket to pale blue-gray, I chose a delicate flower print for the shoulder and back panels and then searched for pastel colored buttons and trims to decorate the cuffs, waistband, and pockets. Any of the materials mentioned in the "what to save" list (page 30) make good patch material, but don't forget, for strength, to use the fabric doubled.

If you are patching an area for super strength, knees or the seat of the pants, for example, there are several additional techniques to consider. The first is to use a commercial iron-on patch on the inside of the garment for durability, and then for fun, sew a decorative appliqué on the outside, covering the repaired area. This is how the child's pants were done. They will wear well, but the iron patches will never soften like the denim and many people find this eternal stiffness annoying.

Another good patch source is denim salvaged from a retired pair of jeans. The fabric, with softened fibers and washed out colors (preferably to contrast somewhat in both color and weight) can look terrific as a repair.

If you prefer to use regular doubled cotton from your scrap collection, try quilting a pattern into the appliqué patch. The quilting adds tremendous strength to the tired fabric underneath because it joins the patch to the original surface in so many places.

an appliqué knee patch   *an appliqué knee patch*

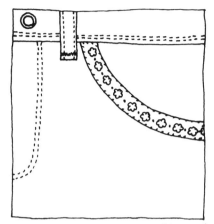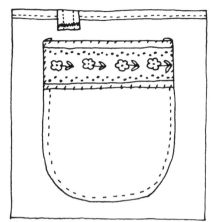

using ribbon to repair frayed pockets

Ribbon, added as a single strip or as a block, makes a great patch material. It is strong and has woven edges which eliminate hemming. Use it to cover minor injuries or sew pieces together to cover a large hole.

Areas like weakened seams, frayed necks and pockets, and raveled cuffs can be covered and reinforced easily and beautifully with ribbon because there are no edges to turn under except the cut ends of the ribbon. But make sure the trim you use is washable.

Lengthening Jeans

Cotton denim is a living, breathing, changing fabric. It is because of these qualities that jeans are so comfortable to wear. But this "life" also has its drawbacks. Not only can jeans shrink and stretch to conform to the body contours, they can also shrink and become too short. Learn to cope with this practically unavoidable event and you will extend the life of your pants. Of course you could avoid this problem altogether by constantly having them dry-cleaned or handwashing them in cold water, but this seems out of keeping with the spirit of denim. Assuming you will be treating your jeans in workaday fashion, there are several ways they can be lengthened.

If your jeans just need an extra inch or two, heavy-duty washable ribbon will do a terrific job. Decide what width of ribbon you will need and then choose a pattern that blends well with

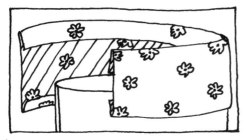

lengthening jeans: wrapping fabric

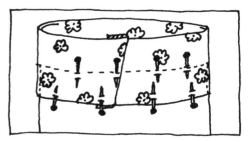

pinning in position

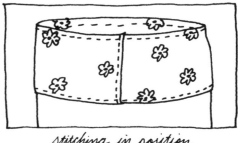

stitching in position

denim. Pin the ribbon in place around the bottom of each pants leg, turn under the cut end, and machine stitch in place. Choose a ribbon that is wider than the actual distance to be lengthened so the ribbon can be attached with a significant grip on the denim.

Ribbon can also be used the same way as patch material to neaten and reinforce frayed cuffs and pockets. Since you will be expecting the ribbon to go through the same washings and dryings as the denim, be sure to use a superior quality of ribbon.

If your jeans need more extreme lengthening, consider using cotton fabric doubled. Cut the fabric to twice the necessary width and fold it in half. Pin it in place around the bottom of the jeans with the folded edge along the bottom. Fold under the top edge ¼ inch as shown, pin in position, and machine stitch.

Decorating with a Theme—Daniel's Denim Jacket

Daniel's denim jacket on the next page is decorated with ducks. A swimming duck is appliquéd on the back panel; the cuffs, collar and waistband are trimmed with running duck ribbon; and a

decorating with a theme :
jean jacket for Daniel

front pocket and panels are covered with duck buttons splashing over rickrack waves. Children's jackets are especially wonderful to work on because often, as on Daniel's jacket, there are easy-to-reach, great-to-decorate patch pockets. But the fun of decorating and the concept of tying together your trimmings with a consistent theme such as flowers or animals can easily be applied to an adult-sized jacket. There are so many styles of denim jackets available that you will have to decide where patching will be most effective.

The duck scene on the back of Daniel's jacket is cut, hemmed, pressed, and sewn in place according to the appliqué instructions on page 44. The duck's silhouette and the outside edge of the pond are buttonhole-stitched with green embroidery floss. The duck's eye is a bead, the rust color ripple he floats on is rickrack, and the stripe below it is flowered ribbon. All the ribbon, including that on the collar, cuffs, and waistband, was pinned in place and machine stitched along each edge.

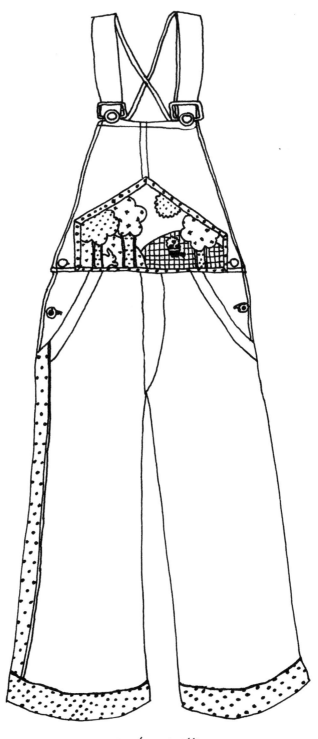

work overalls

Work Overalls

Work overalls, also reliable friends, deserve to be decorated with whimsical trim to help them lead a fuller life or patched artfully when they begin to fail. Brenda created an elegant pair when she covered the bib of white-duck painter's overalls with an enticing brown gingham and flowered country pasture complete with trees, birds, and a woven rickrack basket of freshly harvested hearts. Dotted ribbon gaily reinforces the outside seams and brown checked cuffs lengthen the legs.

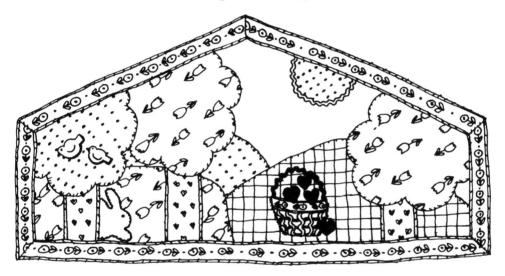

flowered country pasture

I wanted to make myself an overall dress. I experimented with a child size because the waist measurement was close to my own. Even though the pants legs were much too small when the overalls were intact, once they were cut and patched into a skirt, the garment had an easy fit, especially at the waist and hips. If you plan to make an overall jumper for yourself or someone with a small waist, consider using a child's size too. They run to size 16.

The remarkable thing about this transformation is that even if you have but a brief acquaintance with the sewing machine, it still takes less than an hour to have a new jumper. This technique, by the way, is also great for converting jeans into skirts.

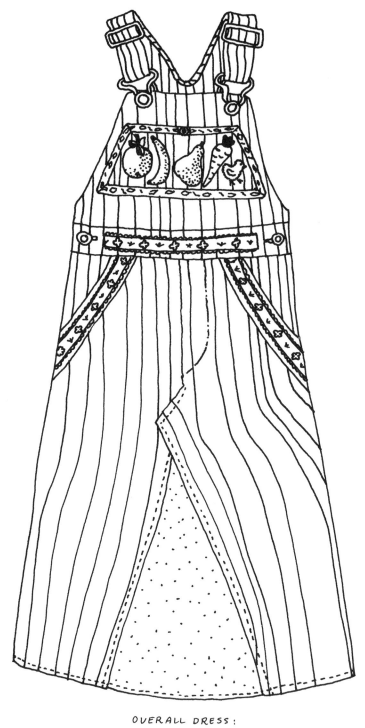

OVERALL DRESS:

*the same method can also be
used for making a jeans skirt*

The overalls I used were navy and white striped and the triangular patches were navy denim. I covered the bib with commercial appliqués using fruits and vegetables and a little chick. If you want to use these ready-made shapes effectively, try choosing a theme of fruits, flowers, or hearts. By keeping to simple shapes and consistent colors (like all deep tones or all pastels) you will have a head start in creating a strong visual picture. Using primary colors, I sewed flowered ribbon across the waistband by machine (because it fitted through easily) and around the pockets and bib by hand (because they were hard to get at).

decorated bib using commercial appliqué

To make the skirt, cut straight up the inside seam of one pants leg, up again to within an inch of the fly (but not through it!) and down the inside seam of the other leg. Next put the overalls on the floor back side facing up (might as well practice on the back), and gently fan the legs into a sloping skirt. Up near the fly, where there are those extra bits of fabric, I overlapped the pieces. This trick magically allows the skirt to lie flat by creating a tuck.

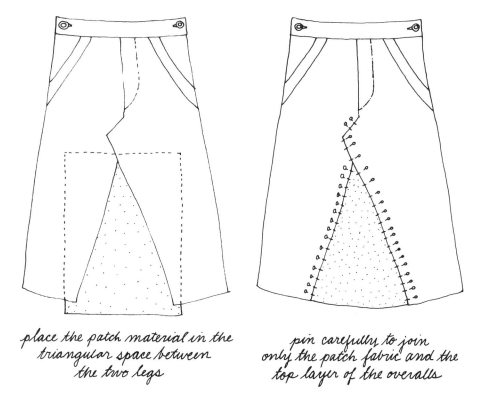

place the patch material in the triangular space between the two legs

pin carefully to join only the patch fabric and the top layer of the overalls

Place the patch material, which should be just wider than the bottom open edge of the triangle, in the triangular space between the two legs, just under the top surface of the overalls. Turning the cut overall edges under, so they don't fray later, pin carefully to join only the patch fabric and the top layer of overall legs. If you work from the crest of the triangle and down each side, easing the fabric as you work, the overall legs should pleasingly cover the patch. When you are satisfied that there are no bulges, run the pinned work through the sewing machine. Remove the pins, turn the garment over, and repeat. Don't forget to overlap that extra flap of fabric on the second side too.

If the overall length is satisfactory for you as a dress (mine was at mid-calf), trim the patched areas leaving fabric allowance, turn under, and hem with double machine topstitching to match the finished edge already there.

If you want to shorten the dress, measure with a yardstick from the floor, and evenly trim off any excess fabric. Hem with a double row of machine topstitching to keep the heavy-duty denim flavor.

BIBLIOGRAPHY

Edwards, Phoebe. *The Mountain Mist Blue Book of Quilts.*
Cincinnati, Ohio: Stearns and Foster, date not given.

Emery, Betsy, ed. *McCall's How to Quilt It.*
New York, New York: The McCall's Pattern Co., 1953.

Gonsalves, Alyson Smith, ed. *Quilting and Patchwork.*
Menlo Park, California: California Lane Publishing, 1973.

Ickis, Marguerite. *The Standard Book of Quiltmaking and Collecting.*
New York, New York: Dover Publications, 1949.

Lane, Rose Wilder. *The Woman's Day Book of American Needlework.*
New York, New York: Simon and Schuster, 1963.

Laury, Jean Ray. *Quilts and Coverlets, A Contemporary Approach.*
New York, New York: Van Nostrand Reinhold, 1970

Safford, Carleton, and Bishop, Robert. *America's Quilts and Coverlets.*
New York, New York: E. P. Dutton and Co., Inc., 1972.

Wooster, Ann-Sargent. *Quiltmaking, The Modern Approach to a
Traditional Craft.* New York, New York: Drake Publishing, 1972.